Reviews and Readers' Comments

"If you are thinking of moving to Hawaii you must buy this book!

Affordable Paradise begins with the realities of living in Hawaii. Hawaii is different from the mainland, and this section discusses attitudes, ways of living, if your kids will get picked on in school, crime, and most importantly, lays out for you what will probably be the hardest parts about living in Hawaii.

You will learn about homes and land unique to Hawaii, and then go on a whirlwind tour of the Big Island, noting the quirks and environments of each area and many subdivisions. You'll then learn the ins and outs of actually moving to Hawaii: what you should bring, what won't last long here, and how you can get your stuff over. Finally, the subject of how you can make your living and stretch your dollar is addressed. Retired? There is a section for you too. I moved here from the mainland, and I can tell you from experience— *Affordable Paradise* is right on."

Melissa Weber
AndHawaii.com Hawaii Travel Information

"I really enjoyed *Affordable Paradise*. The tone of your writing conveys the deep appreciation you have for Hawaii. If other readers find your enthusiasm to be as contagious as I did, you're on your way to a very popular title."

Pelin Thornhill
Editorial Assistant *Lonely Planet Publications*

"Bravo on Affordable Paradise! I just received mine last week and thought it was beautifully done!

Thank you so much for putting out such a well-written, factual straight-to-the-point book on moving to the Big Island. Hope this finds you healthy and happy!

L. S., Los Angeles, CA

"This is the best book on moving to Hawaii I have encountered to date. My husband and I have been visiting Hawaii for the last 6 years with the hope of one day moving there.

Your book described exactly our feelings about the islands and our desire to be part of the culture and aloha spirit that is Hawaii. When we visit Hawaii, we become entirely different beings immersing ourselves in everything that the islands have to offer. We are not the same people that we are here in the Midwest, and that is just fine with us.

Thanks again for the wonderful wealth of information in your book. We look forward to being island residents soon."

E. J., Naperville, IL

"*Affordable Paradise* caught my attention from the introduction and the almost spiritual first chapter. The next chapters took me gently into the realities [of Island living] in an honest and very detailed manner. A lot of things are covered that we simply never thought about. In spite of the realities, some of which may make some folks reassess their plans, for us, you guided us back to the conclusion that a move and the subsequent "simplifying our life", was not only doable but very desirable. We are comfortable in the knowledge that we are making our decision based upon what seemed like reading a letter from a caring friend. Congratulations! For us you have really conveyed the "ALOHA SPIRIT", and we are looking forward more than ever to our exploratory trip and our final move."

Denis and Mary Ann, Washington State

Wow, I was hoping for exactly what your book provided and I plan on reading it again after my wife gets a chance. Thanks again and enjoy your paradise as we hope to now enjoy ours.

Dave and Peggy, South China, Maine

Affordable Paradise

The Secrets of an Affordable Life
in Hawaii

H. Skip Thomsen

Oregon Wordworks
Portland, Oregon 97281

Affordable Paradise
The Secrets to an Affordable Life in Hawaii

By H. Skip Thomsen
Edited by Camille Thomsen

Cover art, layout, and design by the author.
All photographs by the author, except as noted.

Published by:
OREGON WORDWORKS
P.O. Box 231091, Portland, OR 97281
www.mailbooks.com

Printed in the USA

Limits of Liability and Disclaimer
This book is based on years of experiences and observations of the author and the many people interviewed during the writing process. The author shall not be held liable in any event for incidental or consequential damages in connection with or arising out of the use of information contained in this book.

Table of Contents

Acknowledgements

I wish to express my gratitude to the entirety of the Island of Hawai'i: her many people who have both knowingly and unknowingly contributed to the creation of this book; her awesome *Mana*, A*ina and Aloha,* without which there would have been no need for this book; and to my bride, Camille, who gave her unfailing assistance in every phase of the project.

Mahalo Nui!

Skip Thomsen

Introduction

There are already books that will tell you all about moving to Hawai'i and how expensive it is to live here. They'll tell you that the median house price is $350,000 and that you had better be well off if you plan to live in Paradise. Even without the books, anyone who has ever visited the Islands already "knows" that Hawai'i is one of the costliest places to live.

We're now going to show you how this isn't necessarily the case. We'll reveal how anyone with the desire to do so can indeed afford to live in Paradise!

Our Paradise is the Big Island; the Island of Hawai'i. The Big Island is a place of awesome beauty and incredible variety. To many folks, us included, the Big Island is exactly what we came to Hawai'i to experience. Especially on the lush, tropical Windward (Hilo) side, the pace of life is gentle and easy, the weather is perfect and the air is sparkling clean.

The prices you might see in other publications are intimidating to all but the well-to-do. You'll read how if you're lucky, you might find a small starter-home in need of repairs for $200,000. You'll be told to expect to pay at least $800 a month for a tiny one-bedroom apartment.

Here on the Big Island, it's a world apart from the above scenario. Many homes for sale here are in the $100,000 range and there are some very livable smaller homes for half that amount.

If you have around $700 a month budgeted for rent, you'll have your choice of many lovely homes, some right in the city and others as far away from the city as you would like.

Hard to believe? We'll prove it to you. We'll not only share with you the secrets of affordable living in Hawai'i, but also tell you how to plan your move and then how to get the most for your money in every facet of your day-to-day Island life.

But before we jump in and start looking for that new home, please understand that this book is not an effort to sell Hawai'i to the masses. It is as much to discourage those who would not be at ease here as it is to encourage those to whom Hawai'i could forever be their home.

To that end, we strive to present both sides of the picture. We won't tell you that Hawai'i is everyone's Paradise, because clearly, it is not. But for those who are at peace here and who yearn from their hearts and souls to live here, we offer ways to make it possible and affordable. You can live in Hawai'i on a modest income, and we're about to show you how.

Chapter One

The Dream

Aloha is alive and well!

There's a magical, special feeling in these Islands of Hawai'i. Those of us who live here call it *Aloha*. It's alive and well, and to some it's so powerful and pervasive that it soon becomes an essential part of life. To many people, this feeling is exactly what they're here for. Perhaps they're even here for healing or for a specific spiritual focus, but in any event it's the mystique and power of the Islands that brings them to this extraordinary destination in the first place, and in the end it is what keeps them here forever.

To others, these feelings seem not to exist. We've had friends from the mainland come to visit and notice nothing, while others feel it profoundly. We even had one friend say that she surely feels the ambiance of love and acceptance here but she thought it was some kind of tourist-trickery being played by the Visitor's Bureau! And she was serious!

The more obvious draw of this Island is its natural resources: the pristine beaches, the crystal clear ocean, the awesome and varied flora, and of course the spectacular volcano. A less obvious but no less important draw is the *mana*, or spiritual power. The big Island is home and host to many spiritual events, sessions, celebrations, and workshops from many differing disciplines. The Zen Temple in Wood Valley hosts these kinds of events all year long, and others take place in less formal surroundings, like in some of the sacred and powerful places all over this Island or perhaps even on a quiet beach. The Magic here is one of the big reasons why so many people are drawn here for their spiritual work. It's somehow so easy here.

Each of us sees "the Dream" differently. To some, it's being able to spend lots of time on beautiful white sand beaches and never again having to think about "going back home." To others, it's the sumptuous weather and never again having to burn anything to keep warm. Or it's the quiet, gracious, simple and unhurried lifestyle. And to others still, it's as simple as this: It feels good. It feels good to every one of our senses, psychological, physical and spiritual.

To us, it is all of these things. It is somehow so easy and natural to stay grounded here, and there is just "something in the air" that is a constant, gentle reminder that keeps us on our spiritual path. This is a simple life where friends matter more than timetables, where inner peace and *Aloha* come easy.

It feels so good to us to be among these wonderful people of many cultures who all seem to be of one big, loving family. The color of your skin, the kind of car you drive, the size of your home—none of these things matter here. What's in your heart is all that matters.

Have you ever noticed how even in the big city, everything and everyone seems somehow different right around Christmastime? People just seem to be friendlier, more inclined to take the time to say hello to strangers. It's like that all year long here.

This is a generalization, but we believe those who end up staying here are the people who Know in their Knowingness the minute they first breathe the sweet, sensuous air of the Islands that they have come home and that this is where they must be.

The Change to Island-Style

It's interesting to observe our new friends and neighbors as they fall into step with Island life. It's especially interesting to watch the women who came from a professional life in some big city. At first, they find it awkward to shed the all-important apparel they've become so used to and adapt the comfortable attire of the Islands. It's not too long, though, before they find real pleasure in their new comfort of pareos and rubber slippers. Even the makeup that was an everyday routine starts to become less important, and before long, it isn't needed any more at all.

Men, too, take a while to adapt. But pretty soon the rubber slippers and shorts feel natural and they can laugh at the clothes they used to wear to keep up with the styles in the city. And then they wonder why it took so long.

Another interesting observation is how most people simply slow down. Those who talk fast, move fast and come from life in the fast lane are the most dramatic to watch. From the frenetic pace they brought with them, they begin the beautiful and healthy process of slowing down every nuance of their lives. Speech slows down and becomes more focused, mannerisms become more graceful and at ease, attention to others becomes more deliberate and loving, and they begin, consciously or not, to live *Aloha*.

The People

In the Islands, and particularly in the rural areas, people always have time for friends, neighbors and even strangers. There's a popular pastime here called "talk story." You always have time to talk story. If you're ready to leave your home to go on an errand and a friend shows up, you stop what you're doing and talk story. You share a cup of coffee, tea or whatever, but you always have time. That's why sometimes appointments seem to have little meaning here. The bottom line is that people are more important than anything else.

Speaking of people, one of the things we love about living here is that everybody is a minority. There is no prejudice here; what your personal culture is doesn't matter. Again, it's what's inside that counts. This is especially true here on the Windward side of The Big Island, where the population is a wonderful mix of Hawai'ian, Chinese, Japanese, Filipino, Portuguese, *haole* (Caucasian), different Island cultures and others, and the beautiful results of the mixes of all of them.

There is an obvious respect for everyone's culture, and each practices it's own ways to whatever extent they wish. And for those who have heard stories of how "the locals all dislike *haoles*" and other exceptions to this notion, we'll discuss that in Chapter 2.

The Hawai'ian culture is alive and well here, and is being preserved and nurtured. It's truly heartwarming to us every time we see another example of the energy that the young people here, especially the Hawai'ian kids of all ages, put into the preservation of their culture. The Hawai'ian culture is built upon love and acceptance, family and friends, the land and the ocean, and to a large extent, the *Hula* and music. These are the important things; everything else is secondary. There are lots of Hawai'ian cultural events here, and we recommend attending as many as possible. It's good to continue to learn about the culture and the ways of the people who are our hosts here in these Islands, and to maintain the highest possible respect for this amazing place and its people.

The cultural events we speak of are those put on by the local folks. There are theater events, street parties, talks by Hawai'ian elders, museums, musical events of all descriptions and even small *Luau*s and other informal gatherings where you can learn about local ways by observation and becoming involved. With a few exceptions, the so-called cultural productions by hotels and other tourist endeavors are not among our recommendations for really learning about Hawai'ian ways or history.

A large part of the Hawai'ian culture is based in the philosophy of giving back to the community. Those who live this philosophy would feel incomplete living their lives only for themselves, or even just for their own families. The family as a whole gives back to the community, and this, coming from the heart, is an important ingredient of the spirit of *Aloha*. This is a philosophy not often found to be practiced in Mainland *haole* cultures and it is one of the differences not easily understood by the Hawai'ians. Not surprisingly, the Island *haole*s who truly live lives of *Aloha* are those who find themselves most at ease with—and accepted by—the locals.

The dream of living in these Islands has as many interpretations as there are dreamers, and no one interpretation is less real than any other to the one doing the dreaming. There are few places on Earth that cast this kind of spell on their guests. If you are one of the dreamers, take heart! If it is truly your desire, you can live that dream.

Hilo as seen from Coconut Island (Cover Photo)

Chapter Two

The Realities

E very day, folks come here and are enchanted by the magical feelings of these Islands, and some decide they just have to live here. Some of them decide too soon. They pack their belongings into a shipping container and move on over, and in a few months or maybe a year, they discover that this isn't "America." It's really much more like living in a foreign country, with a very different culture, and that culture comes with a different attitude and a different energy than that of most places on the Mainland. A lot of the locals here refer to the Mainland as "America," and prefer to think of the Hawai'ian Islands as a separate country. Their separate country. Not wishing to get into a lengthy political discussion here, there are certainly lots of good and valid reasons for their preference.

We use the term "locals" to refer to the people who have lived in the Islands for most or all of their lives. Locals can be of any culture or race, too, and that even includes *haole*.

In many ways, some subtle and others not-so-subtle, things work differently here. If the way they work fits in with your temperament, there's a good chance you'll find Hawai'i to be your special place. It's a very laid-back lifestyle, and if you can live with that and love it, it's a good start. But there's much more to it than that.

Indeed, it is the "laid back" part that attracts a lot of folks at first, but then in the end it can be some of the ingredients of "laid back" that seem to be their undoing.

This is a Test . . .

In this chapter we're going to share a few of the reasons some people turn tail and head back for the Mainland after trying Island life for a while. It has been suggested we leave out this chapter; that it is too negative. Well, that's why it's called "The Realities." Actually, it's rare when two or more people who observe the same situation come away with the same "reality," and your own reality of life in Hawai'i will be yours alone. Much depends on your own values and perceptions, so what we are sharing in this chapter are some of the things you need to "feel" for yourself. If the situations and word pictures we conjure up feel good to you, that's great. If they don't, we recommend a thoughtful evaluation on why not. If they don't feel good now, will they become major irritations later? Life in rural Hawai'i is not the same as a vacation at Waikiki Beach, and we would like you to be able to make a decision that will keep you smiling for a very long time.

A little story

Is the Dream real? How do we know if the dream is real or if we are just temporarily infatuated with the lure of the Islands?

A few months ago, we met a woman who had recently bought this beautiful home on a nicely manicured acre of tropical forest. She was fresh over from the Mainland and apparently quite taken with the property when she looked it over several times before the purchase, and appeared to be really excited about her decision to move to Hawai'i. She went back home, had all her belongings packed and shipped over and arrived in her new home. The sellers had left it immaculately clean, with gorgeous flowers everywhere. There were even orchids floating in the toilets, a kind of *Aloha* tradition. The sellers had also made her a gift of quite a bit of furniture to ease her transition and make her comfortable until her container arrived.

Much to our surprise, it wasn't a month later when we heard her start complaining about a few things. Some things about the house, the location, the rain in particular and the weather in general. When she started in on the people, we knew she wouldn't be here long. Everywhere she went, she came upon "that local attitude," mostly because people didn't do things the way she had come to expect from her Mainland experiences. Eventually, she became bitter about nearly everything, and now her dream house is for sale and she's on her (disillusioned) way back to America. This is not an isolated incident.

Different place, same problems

Many of us who are troubled by one thing or another seem to feel that a change of scenery will somehow fix everything. Maybe it's the hectic pace of city life, family problems, a boss we have trouble relating to, or just some restlessness. Sometimes a change of scenery might be all it takes for us to get ourselves grounded and be able to function at a new level that makes positive changes in our lives. But too often, we tend to bring the old baggage with us. The new place feels really great for a while . . . while it's still new. Then pretty soon, the things that somehow fascinated us at first start to irritate us and we begin unpacking that old baggage. Before we know it, we're trying—most likely at a subconscious level—to make the new place more like the old place, and before we know what's really happening, the frustration starts all over just like it did before.

It's really important that we seek our new environs for the right reasons. Ideally, we don't do it as an escape, but rather as a move to some place that feels even better than where we are now. Well, that's the ideal way. It's kind of like hooking up with a new partner; if you're coming from an insecure, needy place, you're not likely to be moving into an aspiring new relationship.

We would like to think of your move to Hawai'i as adding a brilliant rainbow to your already beautiful, bright blue sky.

Since it's probably unreasonable to assume that all of us will be in so enviable a space in our lives, let's go to a more likely scene: We're wage-slaves in a big city, making lots of money and spending it faster than we're earning it. We can feel in our hearts the shallow existence of working so hard just to be able to keep paying the bills that let us afford to keep working. We know that there's something better out there; that this is not what we were put here for. Then one day, we decide to take a vacation to Hawai'i, and when we step off the airplane and take our first breath of Hawai'ian air, we just know in all of our being that we have just come home—that this is where we must be.

We spend the next few days nearly overwhelmed with the beauty of everything, that magical, mystical feeling that is so pervasive and just makes us want to hug everyone. We breathe that sweet, sensuous air, swim in the caressing, crystal-clear ocean; feast on sumptuous tropical fare, and just drink in the essence. We're hooked!

This is what happens to a lot of folks; it's what happened to us. But if it goes far enough that we start to consider actually relocating to Hawai'i, it's time to feel the lifestyle in its entirety.

A Peaceful Existence . . . Challenged

There are many ingredients to this peaceful existence, and they mostly revolve around a general attitude that people are more important than things, profits or time-tables. A simple example of this is the "talk story" story we told you earlier. You don't even consider saying to your neighbor that you are just on your way out; you invite her in, fix her a cup of coffee and you listen to what she came to tell you, or if it was nothing in particular, you just enjoy the Now of each other's company for awhile. You don't take those periodic Mainland-style glances at your watch. You don't even own a watch! In due time, she leaves and you head for your friend's place, arriving some time in the early afternoon. Your friend doesn't ask why you're "late," because outside the realm of business appointments, "late" is kind of a foreign concept here and not often considered.

In personal relationships, this works better than in business arrangements, but it still happens there, too. A contractor might simply not show up for the job he said he'd do, because the surf was particularly good that day and no way was he going to miss it. This is understood here to a certain level and accepted by many. There is a point at which it's not very nice to space out a business commitment, and this is exactly the point where you'll find that those who keep their commitments are the ones who are never looking for work.

The key, of course, is to be at peace with this lifestyle, and if that comes naturally to you and feels very good to you, you'll probably do well here. If it feels like it will take all the patience you can muster to put up with the leisurely ways of the Islands, then this might not be your cup of tea.

This casual attitude is pervasive here, and it's just part of life. It drives some people up the wall, and others fall into a comfortable step with it. It's important to would-be residents that they be honest enough with themselves to know that their acceptance of this kind of lifestyle is real and not just fun because it's new. Folks who have spent a good part of their lives on the Mainland big-city treadmill or living a life of appointments and timetables might have difficulty adjusting. If you feel uneasy about the adjustment, we strongly suggest renting for a while before making a commitment to live in Hawai'i.

Leaving Behind Family and Friends

Another issue we recommend for serious consideration is that of leaving behind family and friends. We've heard from dozens of families and individuals who put everything they had into moving to Hawai'i, only to return to the Mainland in a year of two because they could not deal with the distance between themselves and their families.

Grandparents seem to have the biggest problem with it, too. Just yesterday, we were at a garage sale in our little community and met these folks for the first time as they were selling their belongings in preparation for their move back to the Mainland. We asked them why they were moving, and they replied, "We need to be close to our grandbabies."

Sometimes it is grandkids, others it will be kids, parents, grandparents, or even friends.

We have kids over there, too, and we miss them terribly. But in this mobile society of ours, we could conceivably move back to California to be closer to them just as they decide to move to Florida.

We've thought long and hard on these issues, and have come to the conclusion that Hawai'i is where we must be for our own peace and happiness. We worked for many years to be able to now live our dream; a modest lifestyle in the one place on the planet we love best. It is also our kids' option to live where they choose, and they just happen to choose a different place. We still see them, although not nearly as often as we'd like. Although it wasn't an easy choice, we have made the conscious decision to live with it this way, and always silently hope that at least some of them will eventually join us here.

Other people handle it in different ways. One couple we know moved back a little over a year ago because they felt that need to be closer to their kids and grandkids. After spending the better part of a year back in Oregon learning that their kids had busy, active lives and that they hardly ever had any time to share with their parents, this couple said the heck with this, we're going back! They subsequently made the same decision we did and are here to stay.

We've heard this same story from others, too. After going back, we hear they don't see the kids any more living there than they did when they lived here, and furthermore, when they lived here and the kids came to visit, there was more quality time than when the parents tried to fit into the kids' busy schedules on the Mainland.

It isn't always like that, though. Some people simply cannot tolerate such a distance between themselves and loved ones, and it is really important that you take a close look at yourself, your family ties and how well you would do with your family an ocean away. Consider how often you see your kids, your grandkids if you have any yet, parents or other loved ones, and what a difference it would make in all of your lives if you were no longer involved in the same way.

Parents, or even grandparents, present a whole new set of rules, too. With kids, the decision might be a little easier just because everyone involved is mobile. It doesn't take a lot to jet on over to the Islands for a visit. With elderly parents or grandparents, especially those who depend on their families for support in any number of ways, it becomes a different matter.

These are intensely personal issues and need thoughtful, conscious consideration before making plans to relocate to an Island in the middle of the ocean.

If this all sounds like we're now trying to talk you out of living in Hawai'i, please understand that we simply want you to know some of the details that so many before us have had to learn the hard way. Details that weren't even noticed in the newness of life in Paradise, but then for some, metamorphosed into monsters later on. We want you to go into this with your eyes wide open; conscious and aware that this new lifestyle could well be your Paradise, but that it is not for everyone.

One More Challenge

That said, there are other things about living in the Islands that you need to know about in advance of buying a home, and one is the dog thing. For some reason, dogs are popular in all parts of rural Hawai'i. It is not uncommon for people to own four or five dogs. What is uncommon is trained dogs.

We've talked to dog owners whose animals bark day and night and we've asked them what's up with that. "Hey, they're dogs. Dogs bark. That's what dogs do," was our answer.

This problem has become real enough now that it appears on real estate disclosure statements, as well it should. If you are about to buy a home and there is no mention of dogs on the disclosure statement, it would be in your best interest to make sure your real estate agent asks the seller if there are any nuisance dogs in the area.

This is just so that you will be aware of the possibilities, and we recommend a walk around in any neighborhood you may be contemplating moving into. Best to know before you sign on the line. We talk a little more in Chapter 3 about checking for neighborhood dogs while house-hunting.

More on Hawai'i's "High Cost of Living"

The "high cost of living in Hawai'i" is like most things here—true for some and a myth for others. For us, it's a myth. In Chapter 6, we go into the details of how and why this works. Here in our discussion on "realities," we'll prepare you for some of the things that do cost more here and are difficult to get away from.

The main areas of higher-than-Mainland costs are electricity, car and homeowner's insurance, and some specific grocery items. Gasoline is an issue to some who come here from the few places where it's still cheaper, but most recently-from-the-Mainland folks we've talked to say that prices are not much different from those on the Mainland. On the positive side is that most people drive a lot less here than they do on the Mainland where long distances are accepted as normal. Even on the Big Island, the drive from Kona to Hilo, on opposite sides of the Island, is about two hours.

Electricity

Unfortunately, we aren't given any choices here. Unless we use solar or some other alternative to buying our power, we will pay the price. Electricity costs over twenty cents per kilowatt hour in Hawai'i, which is several times the cost of some Mainland areas. California's recent energy problems have put their prices more in line with ours, and this is apparently indicative of the eventual future of electricity prices nation-wide. Certainly that seems to be the trend.

The upside is that unless you live in the mountains, there is no heating required here and air-conditioning is provided by tropical trade winds, so your overall power bill might not be any more than it was on the Mainland. The average monthly residential power bill here is around $100. We have friends who are very frugal and get by with half that figure, but this is the exception. Our bill for a 1200 square foot home averages $125 a month, but much of that is for power tools, computers, a dehumidifier, and other office equipment we keep running a lot. We are also not as frugal as we should be with lights!

Solar, by the way, is a viable, if not attractive alternative here. You'll hear lots of stories about how "solar doesn't work," but those stories are almost always based upon observations of so-called solar systems that were assembled by novices from inadequate components. There are many homes in rural areas here where people rely on these underpowered systems. The systems usually consist of up to four solar panels, an inexpensive (read: inefficient) inverter and a few batteries. They always include a noisy, expensive-to-operate gasoline generator to use when the homeowner needs more power than what will run a few light bulbs.

So the stories usually go like this: Yeah, I've been in a few of those solar homes, and all they have a few dim lights and maybe a couple of 12-volt appliances, and the owners have to constantly fiddle with the system to get it to work.

OK, here's the flip side. There are properly built systems in place here that comfortably run an entire house, year 'round, with no need for a backup generator. What's the catch? The catch is that these systems cost in the neighborhood of $15,000. Yes, that's a pile of money, but if you do the math you'll find the payback is pretty good with the high price of electricity here. Plus as you keep getting your power from the sun year after year, the price of electricity keeps going up for everyone else. Solar components, especially the panels themselves, have dropped in price over the last ten years while becoming dramatically more efficient. Not a bad deal in today's world.

Installing a solar system is something that is best done in the design and construction phase of a new home. It is much easier to design a new home for the most efficient use of light and power—and the panels—than it is to retrofit an existing house.

The phone book will direct you to a number of qualified solar contractors who will be happy to answer all of the questions specific to your needs.

Insurance

Auto insurance premiums here are somewhat higher than Mainland prices, but as with everything else, you just have to shop around. Rates vary a great deal from one company to another, and even from one agent to another. For those over 50 years old, the best rates are through AARP's Hartford connection, which are about the same as mainland rates.

Homeowner's insurance is higher in the lava-risk areas, but contrary to some opinions, it is available from private companies. You will still hear from some realtors and others who should know better that it is still not available in these areas, but the fact is, it is. (We have full-coverage homeowner's policies on our vacation rentals and our home, all of which are in Lava Zone 2.) For a time, the only way you could insure a home in Zones 1 or 2 was through an insanely-expensive state-supplied policy. This is no longer the case. Again, shopping around is the way to keep the costs down.

A note on "lava risk zones." The Big Island is divided up into areas of varying "lava-flow risks." Zones 1 and 2 are the highest, which means that there is at least a theoretical potential for some future lava flows. How you wish to interpret the risk and how it might affect you is up to you. Many folks here seem to all but ignore the implied risks and the building of homes in even the highest-risk areas seems to go on as though there was no risk at all. We live in Zone 2 now and recently moved from Zone 1. Although we don't live in fear of losing our home to a lava flow, we do acknowledge that it could happen. Kind of like earthquakes in California, hurricanes in Florida, wildfires in any forested areas of the country, tornadoes in Kansas and all of the similar risks people live with nearly everywhere. The bottom line: we keep our insurance paid up and then get on with our lives.

More on High Prices

Chapter 6 goes into detail on shopping techniques to keep costs to a minimum, but there are some grocery items that are just high here and there doesn't seem to be any way around that. Milk is one of them. The usual lowest price for milk is $3.79 a gallon. Eggs run $1.50 and up, and curiously, imported eggs are usually cheaper than the ones from local producers. Other items that are really high are just about any Mainland-imported, packaged, processed foods. If you must include things like Sugar-Coated Crunchy-Munchies breakfast cereal in your diet, you can save some money by buying the huge packages at Costco. If you have a large family and a freezer to match, you can save big by buying most of your groceries from Costco. Of course, the best deals on fresh produce are from the local farmer's markets. This applies to the markets on the Hilo side of the Island, but unfortunately, the ones in the Kona area seem to have adjusted their prices for the tourists.

Jobs and "Hawai'i's High Unemployment"

Most people who have ever talked to friends about possibly moving to the Islands have heard the stories about how it's nearly impossible to find work here. The reality is that yes, jobs are scarce. According to the local media, things are improving in this area, but it's still difficult for the average person to find a job, particularly if the applicant has no marketable skills. Chapter 7 tells how you can find the right income opportunities to suit your needs. Key here is that jobs are scarce, but there is no shortage of opportunity. Quite the contrary; opportunities abound!

The People, and "That Local Attitude"

Some friends of ours are a family of several cultures. The parents have adopted several mixed-culture children and on the Mainland where they lived years ago, the kids were always taking various forms of harassment for their ethnic diversity. Imagine siblings, black, white and American Indian, all in the same grade-school arena. They moved to Hawai'i when Dad accepted a position at a school in Hilo and their lives changed in a most beautiful way. They found that nobody noticed their differences any more! For the first time in their lives together, these kids were accepted for who they were, and the parents had the good fortune to see their children blossom emotionally and spiritually!

The same thing holds true to a great degree between *haole*s and locals. It's what's in your heart that counts. We've heard all sorts of stories from folks who had been here on vacation or had even lived here for awhile about how "locals all dislike *haoles*" and how difficult it is for a *haole* to get anywhere here because of this alleged discrimination. So over the years, we've observed how this seems to work. It feels to us that most of the locals, particularly those of Hawai'ian ancestry, can see auras. They Know immediately if a person in their midst is there in love or if that person has a pre-conceived notion that generates fear or some other negative emotion in themselves. In our experience, this is a place where the old saying, "you get back what you put out" really holds true.

OK, a little while ago, we mentioned that locals are the folks—including *haoles*—who have lived here most or all of their lives, and now we're talking about locals not liking *haoles*. Confusing? After you've been here for a while, you will easily know the difference between a local *haole* and a newcomer *haole*. It is the newcomer *haole* who gets into trouble. Actually, it's the newcomer, and s/he doesn't need to be a *haole*, either. It's that "*malihini* (newcomer) attitude!"

We've known more than a few folks who fled back to the Mainland mostly because they "couldn't handle the local attitude." Well, our observation has been quite consistent: these people expected that things would happen the way they did "back home," and when they didn't, their exasperation, anger or whatever, came across loud and clear and was met by what they call "that local attitude."

On a few occasions, we observed somebody who would walk into a public office, like maybe the County Building, with a visible chip on his shoulder going in. The local person who had to deal with this customer might then come across as being less than cooperative, or worse, actively uncooperative. An effective way of guaranteeing the appearance of "that attitude" is to tell the local person you're dealing with, "you guys are sure behind the times and in Texas, we do it this way."

We've gone in to those same public-office folks and instead of walking in and arrogantly demanding that our will be done, we approach with a bit of humility and *Aloha*, and ask for the person's help. We have never been mistreated and have always received what we considered to be respectful, helpful cooperation. Any time we have not been greeted with exemplary performance from someone in the business arena, it has been from their lack of knowledge or experience, not out of any attitude problem. The difference is when we ask for help, we do just that: ask for help. We do not go to someone and demand that they serve us—our way. It really does make a difference.

The reason we put so much emphasis on this is because it is worth considering if you are contemplating a life in Hawai'i. Things do work very differently here, and if you are able to love and embrace the Island ways, you will do well. If this sort of difference will be an irritation to you, you will not be happy here.

A recent bumper sticker sighting: "We don't give a _____ how they do it on the Mainland."

More on "the attitude"

There is another aspect of "that local attitude" that needs to be addressed, too. As in most places on our planet, there are always the few who can spoil things for many. Sometimes it's as simple as the few who will throw trash out of their cars, spoiling the beautiful scenery for many. Other times, it gets worse and the effect on others can be significant. Some areas of the Island seem to attract more than their share of these people whom we like to refer to as "unconscious." The Puna District is one of these areas. You need to know that the incidents of drug and alcohol abuse, domestic violence and other crimes are higher in some areas of this district than in most other areas of the Island. The Virtual Tour (Chapter 4) identifies some of these areas.

Efforts are being made to clean up the problems, and the results of the efforts are usually directly proportional to the willingness of the individual members of the communities to get involved. "Neighborhood Watch" programs have proven to be very effective in maintaining safe, quiet communities. It is necessary for the community at large to send a clear signal that improprieties will not be tolerated.

We have been told by a number of Police Department folks, including the Chief himself, that the Island Way has always been this: The Police tend to "look the other way" at improprieties occurring in any neighborhood where the community seems to condone such activity. This may seem really strange to somebody from the Mainland where the laws are generally enforced no matter where you might live.

Let's try to look at it from the standpoint of a slowly-evolving Island culture. Now we're looking at a little community where petty mischief has always been common and tolerated by the residents. The mischief might include minor burglaries, like kids entering a home and helping themselves to sodas and snacks when nobody is home. Maybe they've even taken a surf board or two. There are also lots of barking dogs—way more than most folks used to living in quiet communities would consider bearable. Perhaps there's also a slightly obnoxious alcoholic and maybe even a family known to be doing drugs. None of these issues is annoying enough to the residents to do anything about, so life goes on and it seems OK to those who live there. This little village has never really been any different and nobody cares.

Then over the years, a few people from the Mainland come over here and find this area so beautiful that they decide to buy a lot, build a house and call it home. After the initial love-affair with the new surroundings starts to wear off, the "normal" conduct of this village starts to become the focus of the newcomers, and as a few more arrive from the Mainland, the inevitable unpleasant exchanges between the locals and the newcomers begin. (Again, in our discussions here, "locals" refers to anyone who has lived most or all their lives in the Islands. Locals are of all cultures and races including *haole*.) The Police get called about "disturbances" that used to be normal life, the Police talk to the locals and try to smooth things over by asking them to make new compromises to their chosen lifestyle, and they try to explain to the newcomers how this all works. The newcomers interpret the explanation as an unwillingness of the Police to respond to their needs. It isn't. It's just the Police being caught between the proverbial rock and a hard place and doing the best they can. As we've said before, this isn't "America," and it isn't for everyone.

Please know that we are in no way trying to make any judgements about anyone else's lifestyle or the manner in which they choose to live. Just as if we were contemplating moving to a different country anywhere on the planet, the "locals" are our hosts in that country, and it is best if we honor their cultures and lifestyles and either try our best to fit in or seek residence in an area of like-minded souls.

This can be a difficult situation, and we believe it is best handled by checking out any potential areas for your new home very carefully. Drive, or better yet, walk through the community. Do it during the day and at night, as well. Before you decide that this will be your new home, see if the area is mostly local, and if it is, rethink moving there unless you feel very comfortable with the lifestyle you observe there.

What is normal life in many Island communities may not be what you consider normal wherever you come from. It is easy to observe geographic similarities when house-hunting and overlook the cultural dissimilarities. For example, you might drive into a community that because of its beautiful ocean view and the curvy streets reminds you of a special place you've visited on the Mainland. You still need to keep in focus that this is not the Mainland, but that it is much more like a foreign country in many respects. No matter how beautiful or even familiar any particular place feels to you, our suggestions to become as familiar as possible with any areas of interest are still valid.

If you still feel this is where you must be, we strongly recommend renting for at least a few months first. It is quite possible to spend time in some community for a week or two and never be exposed to the very things that will eventually drive you nuts if you lived there.

This Island is so huge and there is so much variety that it is not difficult to find a place where you will be among folks who enjoy a lifestyle much like yours. Just look around, feel each place that calls you, meet some of the people there, go to the stores and get a feel for the local population, and don't be a big rush to settle into one area just because you like the beach there. There's a lot more to it than that!

The Puna District is huge in itself, and not surprisingly, most of the areas needing the greatest vigilance when considering a move are those in the developments with the lowest-cost housing. Check around for a predominance of rented homes. Some developments are mostly owner-occupied and others are mostly month-to-month rentals. If you can't tell by the outside evidence, ask your realtor. The outside evidence includes young-children's toys in the front yards of many of the homes, older and damaged cars, and a general ambiance of neglect. Lots of bed sheets hung as curtains is another good clue. Yes, this is a gross generalization, but it really does apply pretty well to the communities in question. The ones with a lot of rentals generally have the most problems. Again, see Chapter 4 for more specific info.

The Puna District is also one of the most beautiful places on the planet. There are tropical forests, an awesome ocean, bountiful farming land, and any number of other reasons to choose this place as home. Look carefully and thoughtfully, and pick your spot with the clear intention to allow the locals who have been there all their lives to live the way they choose. Please do not move into an area that has what you consider to be social problems and think that you will be able to "fix" them. Remember that what you consider to be problems might be quite normal and acceptable in another's culture. Find the place where the residents already feel as you do about what a community should be all about.

Now let's take all of this to the next level. You've found the perfect place: The people are friendly, those you've met are welcoming you, you don't see any overturned cars or rusted out washing machines in the front yards, there are no snarling dogs, the weather is right, the traffic is light, and the general ambiance of the community feels good.

Now that you have found a place where the people who will be your neighbors are on the same page with you on your ideas of what a community should be like, it's time for that next level, and that next level is you. Are you ready to not only be a good neighbor, but to be a contributing member of your new community? Will you embrace, with a glad heart, the Island Ways we've discussed so far? Are you eager to leave behind those Mainland habits of timetables, deadlines and frenzy?

It's all pretty easy for a while. The challenge seems to be to avoid slipping back into the old ways; to remember never to forget why we're here.

Good beginnings: During your visits to Hawaii, as you contemplate living here, please try to feel deeply the things that attract you, the nuances that make you feel so good about being here. It is so important to remain mindful about these things because it seems, we all tend to forget too easily.

Often, folks come here and are moved by the feelings of *Aloha* they experience everywhere. Maybe it's just a warm smile from a total stranger, a Hawai'ian-style hug instead of a mainland-style handshake, or a gesture such as getting waved into the traffic lane in front of somebody as they wait to leave a downtown driveway on a busy street. But unless they become a part of the *Aloha* community, unless they themselves practice the gestures and habits that moved them to want to live here, they will instead become a part of the

Mainland-attitude community that is diluting the warm and friendly feelings we've been so blessed with.

We feel it is important to our emotional health to take the time for daily reminders of why we're here. Whatever it takes for you, please invest those few moments each day. Sit by the ocean, go for a walk in a rain forest, take in one of the daily spectacular sunsets, breathe deeply the tropical air laced with the aroma of Plumeria. Listen often to the gentle and soothing sounds of Hawaiian music. Attend some Hawaiian cultural events, too. We never leave these events without a renewed love for our Island; a heartfelt love, respect and appreciation for the Hawaiian culture; and a deep feeling of gratitude for the privilege of being able to live here.

Immerse yourself in the company of others who share your appreciation for these awesome Islands. Condition yourself to be conscious of those around you, their needs and their feelings. Reach out to others, give a little here and there. In ways that can only happen in the magical Islands of Hawaii, it all comes back to you many times over.

To those of us who live in the rural areas of the Big Island, the people here are our treasure. Hardly a day goes by that we are not reminded of what we feel to be a perfect ambiance of humanity. We love the ethnic and cultural diversity here, and especially the love and respect—the *Aloha*—that goes on among all of the very different people. Where some people see "scary people," others see friendly, smiling faces. Where some see an attitude, others see love. Different strokes.

These are the kinds of things that any prospective new Hawai'i residents must feel for themselves. The important thing is to be honest about it; honest with yourself. Feel what it feels like to be here among the folks who make their lives happen here; feel the magic, feel the *Aloha*!

This my sound a bit corny, but I would like to share something with you that is very special to me. My bride and I are fortunate enough to live a few hundred feet from the ocean. As I write this, it is early evening, and I'm out on our lanai writing on my laptop. The sky is ablaze with color—brilliant orange to the West and fading into incredible shades of lavender and deep blue over the ocean to the East. All around here are graceful coconut palms, and all this is accompanied by the sounds of the ocean and the gentle guitar of Cyril Pahinui on the stereo. The fading light playing on the breaking waves is awe-inspiring. We are so thankful, every day, for the blessing of being able to live here.

Live *Aloha*!

Waiting for What You Want Right Now!

Another source of frustration for some folks is not being able to get what you want right when you want it. Since many of the goods sold here are imported (nearly all), you get used to waiting for special-order items and you try to make do with what's available now. And even if you feel it's worth the wait, if there happens to be a storm blowing through the shipping channel between the islands, your treasures might just have to wait for next week's shipment . . . even if it's already a week overdue. Just go to the beach . . . all in good time!

Having to wait on special orders can become a real problem for those in business for themselves. We've heard complaints from contractors who had to let hired help go because materials were not on the job in a timely manner. The solution is to plan ahead. That doesn't always work, of course, because there can be unforeseen circumstances that make a mess out of the best plans in the world. But most of the time, careful planning does go a long way toward eliminating this source of frustration. After a while, you learn to anticipate what items will need to be shipped in and you'll make sure they are there when you need them.

For example, we're planning on adding a deck to a rental house in about a month. We know from experience that some of the hardware items we'll need will have to be ordered from the Mainland, so they are already on their way and we'll have them here in plenty of time.

We blew it when we added a new bathroom to our home last year, though. We figured we could get the shower door assembly locally, and we were wrong. We could find only one place on this Island that fabricates non-standard size shower doors, and they wanted so much money for the job that we ended up waiting four weeks to have one shipped from the Mainland. We could have avoided the wait by getting prices way in advance.

For the average person or family, most of what you'll ever need can be found locally. It's good to learn to avail yourself of what is here and make it work in your life. We consider ourselves fortunate to be living a lifestyle that requires little in the way of material goods. This kind of a lifestyle lends itself well to peace of mind, unencumbered lives and budgets that easily stay under control.

Kids and School

There is a definite "pecking order" among the young males in this society. It seems to start in adolescence and go on through—and sometimes a few years beyond—high school. It can be difficult for teens getting transplanted to an Island school, but then it is in any school anywhere, to a point. Here, the transplants seem to subjected to a "proving" period, and during that time they will get tested in various ways. The kids with their self-confidence intact handle it fine; others don't do so well at first, but they always seem to manage sooner or later.

Our son was 14 when he first enrolled in school here, and for his first few months he often came home telling us that he might just never go back. One particular group of about six local guys were giving him "stink-eye," and threatening to "kick his *haole* butt" every time they saw him anywhere. He even avoided going to town with us for fear of encountering these kids. Then one day he had had enough, and all on his own he confronted the bunch of them and told them, "You've been talking about kicking my butt all year.

Now's your chance—start kicking!" For whatever reason, this is all it took for those kids to never hassle him again. Matter of fact, from that day on they were all like old buddies.

We've heard a lot of different variations on this story from other guys who attended high school here. One *haole* friend who grew up in Honolulu and went all through school there said that even though he was one of the star performers on the school's football team, he was still tormented by some of the locals all through school. Then after they graduated, it all stopped as if a hassle-switch had been turned off, and they all became fast friends, which they still are—even after another twenty-five years!

Girls get it, too, but it seems more prevalent, predictable, and sometimes intense with the guys.

The Schools

Big Island public schools have a reputation for being somewhat substandard in scholastic achievement and over-the-top in rowdiness. We don't really have the hard data to refute any of these rumors, and we do hear some of them first-hand ourselves.

We have friends who are teachers, mental-health professionals and counselors at our local high school. They tell us about some of the kids there who don't care about anything besides surfing and getting high. But they also tell us of some of their remarkable kids who are major achievers. At our son's graduation a few years ago, about 60 kids received scholarships. The curriculum is disturbingly easy in what it actually takes to graduate from Hawai'i's schools, and from that point it's not difficult to see why a lot of the young people here have a tough time finding meaningful work when they graduate. The teachers we know of respond enthusiastically to any of their students who seem to be in school to learn (what a concept!), and in spite of the tarnished reputations of some of the schools here, they all produce some outstanding kids. These are the kids whose parents care about them and their education. They are the kids who care about themselves and their futures. Our son graduated from Pahoa High with the means to land a high-paying job as a computer-network specialist in California's Silicon Valley. We know of kids who graduated with University scholarships and others who just barely made it through. A huge part of the difference seems to originate in the homes of the kids, which isn't too much different from kids and schools anywhere.

A relatively new bright spot on the horizon of education are the Charter Schools. Here is some info excerpted from Hawaii's Education Reform Web site (www.edreform.com):

"Charter schools are independent public schools, designed and operated by educators, parents, community leaders, educational entrepreneurs and others. They are sponsored by designated local or state educational organizations who monitor their quality and integrity, but allow them to operate freed from the traditional bureaucratic and regulatory red tape that hog-ties public schools. Freed from such micromanagement, charter schools design and deliver programs tailored to educational excellence and community needs. Because they are schools of choice, they are held to the highest level of accountability - consumer demand.

Charter schools operate from 3 basic principles:

Accountability: Charter schools are held accountable for how well they educate children in a safe and responsible environment, not for compliance with district and state regulations. They are judged on how well they meet the student achievement goals established by their charter, and how well they manage the fiscal and operational responsibilities entrusted to them. Charter schools must and do operate lawfully and responsibly, with the highest regard for equity and excellence. If they fail to deliver, they are closed.

Choice: Parents, teachers, community groups, organizations, or individuals interested in creating a better educational opportunity for children can start charter schools. Local and state school boards, colleges and universities, and other community agencies interested in fostering innovation and excellence in schools sponsor them. Students choose to attend, and teachers choose to teach at charter schools.

Autonomy: Charter schools are freed from the traditional bureaucracy and regulations that divert a school's energy and resources toward compliance rather than excellence. Instead of jumping through procedural hoops and over paperwork hurdles, educators can focus on setting and reaching high academic standards for their students.

Charters provide opportunity for better child-centered education. They provide the chance for communities to create the greatest range of educational choices for their children. Operators have the opportunity and the incentive to create schools that provide new and better services to students. And charters, bound only by the high standards they have set for themselves, inspire the rest of the system to work harder and be more responsive to the needs of the children."

For a thorough look at Hawaii's Charter Schools, please visit their Web site (See Resource Guide).

Crime and Drugs in Hawai'i

Hawai'i doesn't appear to be much different from any other place in the United States when it comes to these issues. Even Paradise has its burglars. And like on the mainland, street drugs are too easily available, and especially to the kids.

There are areas here that seem to have more than their share of crime incidents, and we identify them in Chapter 4.

There are also areas in which any kind of crime is virtually unheard of. We recently moved from a subdivision where we lived for six years. During that time, we never locked a door and always left the keys in our cars. It was a community with an effective "neighborhood watch" program, and it is one of the safest communities on the Island.

The one crime-related issue that bothers us as well as most folks here is that little seems to be done to prevent car break-ins at spots where people regularly gather, like beach parks. There some notorious places here were car break-ins take place nearly daily and several times on a bad day. Ahalanui Beach Park near Pohoiki is one of the worst. The thieves hide in the bushes and wait for an unsuspecting person or family to park. If the culprits observe anything being stashed in a trunk, they wait until the owners are enjoying the beach and for the opportune moment when there's no activity in the parking lot, and then they make quick work out of prying open the trunk and stealing the contents. These cretins think nothing of doing $1000 worth of damage to a car to steal $20 worth of goods from inside. When these thefts are called in to the police, the attitude upon taking the report seems indifferent, at best. We've never personally heard of an arrest or a recovery of stolen goods in any of these cases. In all fairness to the officers who must deal with it, they have expressed their frustration with a system that does nothing to an arrested and convicted individual to deter his continuing this evidently rewarding practice.

So how do we deal with it? When we go to the beaches or any of the problem places, we take our old pickup and leave the doors unlocked and the windows down. Our vehicles have never been bothered. We've actually heard from folks who had their windows smashed when the doors were unlocked. Nobody ever said the burglars were bright.

These occurrences are not unique to Puna or the Big Island. We've had rental cars broken into on Maui and on Kauai when we left them at tourist places and even at our hotels. It is an unfortunate little dark side of our population here, but one that we feel you should know about. You're not likely to hear about it from the Visitor's Bureau. It's really not much different from any other tourist destination, but we want to expect something better from the *Aloha* State.

Politics

We shouldn't even venture into this highly charged topic, but we'll go so far as to give you a heads-up. The political scene just about anywhere on this planet is, unfortunately, a tarnished one. It is no different in Hawai'i. Matter of fact, Hawai'i government, at all levels, has long been famous for its well established good-old-boy systems and its flagrant abuse of the laws, written and implied. Money talks here and the several old, established interests who have forever owned and controlled most of the Islands have the clout to write the laws the rest of us live by and to bend or ignore them as necessary for themselves. Single-interest agendas abound, and politicians regularly make and carry out decisions that are clearly opposed by the large majority of their constituents.

If you like to start your day with the morning paper and you let these kinds of things get to you, you won't be happy here. Because of the small size of the State and its population, the abuses are in your face constantly. Every day our newspapers carry stories that can ruin your morning coffee, if not your whole day. It has been accepted by most people here that Hawai'i is now and always has been run by and for the special interests of the privileged few. Political promises are visibly bought and sold here on a regular basis. Of course, there are always the crusaders and brave souls who put their lives and careers on the line to attempt positive changes, but most of them give up fairly soon.

Elections and campaigns are as shaky as they are anywhere else, but again, because this is a small place and we all get to know our politicians and their records sooner or later, it's all so obvious. Nobody even makes the slightest attempt to hide the nefarious goings on, either.

Again, how do we deal with this personally? We elect to keep ourselves uninvolved from the things we can do nothing about. This is instrumental to our peace of mind. We do make ourselves available to our friends and neighbors, our community and any other individuals and organizations for which we feel we can actually do some good. This is our way of holding onto our peace in Paradise.

Driving Habits

Lots of things are done differently here that can eventually add up to major frustration for some folks. Some of them we've covered above. Another one is a certain local driving style! A few curious Island-style habits (traditions?) take some getting used to. Even more than getting used to them, it takes some amount of acceptance of them if you don't want to be annoyed every time you have to drive somewhere.

If you're from most Mainland areas, you're probably used to driving at or maybe a little above the posted speed limits, right? Well, forget that! Here, the "speed limit" is usually established by someone who chooses to drive at the posted *minimum* speed limit, which on a 55 mph road is usually 45 mph. Nobody seems to know why some people choose to drive so slowly here, but they do, and no matter how many cars are lined up behind them, they don't pull over when they have a chance. They don't take the "slow-moving vehicles" right lane seriously, either. Even some of the slow-moving trucks will simply stay in the left lane through the entire length of a passing lane. The solution is to allow yourself plenty of time to get to where you're going and enjoy the always-beautiful scenery along the way.

There are also some driving habits here that can get you killed if you're not ready for them. One is turns off of a highway. Picture this: You're driving along a two-lane highway (most highways in rural Hawai'i are two-lane) and you're approaching a cross road. The highway traffic has the right-of-way, and there are no right or left turn lanes. The guy in front of you slows down, uses no signals, and as he's slowing, he pulls way to the left side of the traffic lane. He's doing this because he's going to turn left at the cross road, right? Wrong! He's pulling to the far left of the lane because he's going to turn right, and he always turns right from the left side of the road.

OK, now lets rewind the tape to where you're behind this guy, again with no signals going, and he pulls way to the right as he approaches the cross road. Yep, you guessed it. He's going to turn left!

Believe it or not, this happens even if there's a wide enough shoulder that somebody could get completely off of the traffic lane to turn right off of a highway. They'll still take the far left side of the traffic lane and stay there until they've slowed nearly to a stop before crossing the shoulder lane to make that right turn.

This is particularly dangerous to those folks who have moved here from a place where it's common practice to pass to the right side of a car that appears to be waiting to make a left turn. Here, that car might just have slowed to the point where it's about to cross the traffic- and shoulder-lanes to make a right turn.

Please don't get the impression that everybody drives like that here! It's just that it happens enough to be potentially dangerous to folks who aren't prepared for it.

Ready for one more? You're driving along on a 55 mph highway and two or three cars in front of you are going 40. After following them for 15 miles you finally get to a passing lane. Whoopee, right? Right. As soon as the second car is in the passing lane, it pulls to the right of the first one and they stay next to each other through the entire lane, so you're still going 40 at the end of it. It is normal here to ignore passing lanes and just keep driving in the fast lane even if you're puttering along at the minimum posted speed. If you do get a chance to pass in a passing lane, you will most likely have to pass to the right. Even police cars pass to the right in passing lanes, ignoring the person who is illegally ignoring the "slow moving vehicles keep right" signs!

Because of the scenic splendor nearly everywhere, driving in rural Hawai'i can be great. Just remember that it isn't like driving in America. Just take your time and be ever watchful, for the unwritten rules of the road here are different from those you are used to.

A Little Aside

The Hawai'i we're talking about is specifically the Big Island, and then mostly the Windward (Hilo) side of the Big Island. A very different energy exists in other places on the Islands, especially in the heavily-touristed locations. Indeed, Honolulu (on Oahu) is in many ways not much different from being in any number of Mainland cities, except for the year 'round wonderful weather and the white sand beaches. But get lost in the city among all those concrete skyscrapers and traffic jams, and it takes a lot of imagination to remember you're in Hawai'i. Lahaina on Maui is a fun place to visit and play, but again, it's fast-paced, a lot of fast-moving tourist energy, and always party time. For sure, there are a lot of people who wouldn't live anywhere else, but that's not what we're about. For one thing, even if we did want to live there, we couldn't afford it! And to us, these places just aren't what Hawai'i is all about. There's the Hawai'i for the tourists and there's the Hawai'i for living. We're about the Hawai'i for living.

We do cover the more-touristy Kona side of the Big Island because there are folks who enjoy the kind of energy they find there and feel good being in it. It's certainly not anything like Honolulu or even Lahaina, but neither is it like the peaceful, quiet Windward side. Our main focus is on the Windward side.

One way to feel what it will be like living here is to avoid the tourist spots, and instead, rent a condo, apartment or small home in a rural area, in a small community or neighborhood somewhere, or even right in town, as long as it's not a tourist town! You'll find lots of vacation rentals available here by private parties. We own three in our small community and advertise then on the Internet. We go to great lengths to explain to anyone visiting our Web site that this is not a resort; there are no white sand beaches here, no helicopter tours, no *Luaus*, and no souvenir shops! We tell folks that we're a 45-minute drive from town and a long way to everywhere else. Still, a few visitors don't get it and come here and then complain about how hard it is to get to all the tourist facilities! The upside is that the other 99% love it!

What we do offer is a taste of life as it is for those of us who live here, work here and raise our kids here. Those of us who wouldn't live anywhere else. We consider this the "real Hawai'i." You can find many such offerings on the Internet as well as in the local papers, so there's rarely any need to stay in an ordinary (expensive) hotel. (Both of the Island's newspapers are on the Internet and the classifieds are available there as well. See the Resource Guide for addresses.)

We're not trying to invalidate the things that Hawai'i offers tourists! We like to visit Kona and yes, even Lahaina, and play tourist from time to time ourselves, and we thoroughly enjoy doing it. And we certainly do appreciate the need for active tourism here! We just don't want to live there. No doubt lots of folks who love the feeling that is pervasive in the tourist areas like being there better than anywhere else. For them, most of the nuts-and-bolts things we talk about here apply, too. Remember, though, that everything costs more in the tourist areas. Everything, including gasoline, housing, groceries—everything   It's not fair, especially to those who live there year 'round. It's all about marketing: charge what the traffic will bear.

Togetherness

If you are planning to share your Hawai'i experience with your family—or even a partner, the first step is to establish the move as a joint venture. Lack of togetherness can make or break a move, even to Paradise. Togetherness is probably the most important element for a family or couple contemplating any kind of a change of lifestyle, and moving to an Island in the middle of the ocean will be a change even if your are already living a life of *Aloha*.

We've seen situations in which one partner was fully into coming to Hawai'i and the other was just tolerating it. One partner truly felt the call and Knew this was to be home, and to the other, Hawai'i was just another place. A pleasant place with nice weather, but just another place. Even for a single person contemplating relocating to Hawai'i, if this is just another place, no matter how great the warm weather is, we heartily recommend rethinking the move. Again, Hawai'i has the reputation for being a cruel hostess to those who should not be here, and the evidence is the itinerant population, especially on the busy Kona side.

Our neighbors of several years had moved to Hawai'i from Southern California some eighteen years ago. "Robert" loved it here with all his heart and had talked his wife, "Margie," into the move. Margie was never really happy here, particularly since they lived in a community about a 30-minute drive from town. She was used to being able to walk to shopping and she never did stop talking about how she missed all of her old friends. It took eighteen years, but Margie finally got her way and with much sadness on Robert's part, they returned to Southern California.

If you are a family, it's really important to feel out your kids if you're thinking about relocating here. It's important to do that when relocating just about anywhere, but moving to an Island is a pretty radical commitment in many ways, and it is good to have everybody on the same page. Often, kids will seem to love the idea of "moving to Hawai'i!" at first, telling all their friends and loving to watch them all turn green with envy. But then when the time draws near, they seem to grow cold on the whole idea. One way to help ease into the transition, finances and time allowing, is to make a few trips over during the year or so prior to the move, and let the kids feel their way around. Let your kids take you to the places that interest them. If you have settled on a particular area of the Island, take the kids to the school they would attend and introduce them to some of the staff. Often, a staff member or even a student will take your children on a tour through the school. Our son was 15 when we arrived here and a lovely young lady spent nearly an hour taking him through the school and introducing him to some of the students and teachers.

The decision to relocate with school-age children is never an easy one. In some cases, it might be better to wait, especially if your kids have only a year or so of high school to complete. But then there are also the kids who would jump at the opportunity to move to Hawaii, no matter what!

In Conclusion

Hawai'i is not for everyone. Matter of fact, Hawai'i is possibly one of the few places in the country that is so clearly not for everyone. It is said that Hawai'i can reject those who should not inhabit her Islands, and we have known some of her casualties.

It is important to folks contemplating a move to Hawai'i to understand that this is like a different country. The cultures, the lifestyles, the traditions and the basic ways things happen here are all different. And the more rural your lifestyle, the more profound are the differences.

At one extreme, if you lived and worked in Honolulu, you would be well insulated from the differences. But our Paradise is the Big Island, and our biggest "city" is Hilo. Hilo speaks loudly of the differences. Hilo speaks *Aloha*, and those who do not— or cannot—feel this in their hearts will eventually find it difficult to relate here, and in the end will leave. Most won't know exactly why they're leaving—it just won't feel good to be here any longer.

We invite you to do your homework: feel Hawai'i from your heart. Feel what we've shared in this chapter and if any of it makes you uncomfortable, try to find the source of that discomfort.

When you spend time here in Hawai'i and before making the Big Decision, try to feel deeply the things that attract you; the nuances that make you feel so good about being here. It is so important to remain mindful about these things. Many people, it seems, forget too easily.

We see a lot of people who come here and are moved by the feelings of *Aloha* they experience everywhere. Maybe it's just a warm smile from a total stranger, a Hawai'ian-style hug instead of a mainland-style handshake, or a gesture such as somebody stopping for you and waving you into the traffic lane in front of them as you wait to leave a downtown driveway on a busy street.

It feels so good to be in this energy of *Aloha*, but unless each of us is mindful to stay there in our day-to-day lives, it is just too easy to fall back into our hurried Mainland ways. It's too easy to forget the very reasons we decided we had to live here in Paradise.

We've been seeing it happen in our favorite little city of Hilo. Only a few years ago, most of the drivers were courteous, would always be conscious of the needs of others in a traffic situation and try their best to accommodate. You would never have to wait in a driveway for more than a few seconds before somebody would slow down and wave you in ahead of them.

It is happening less now, and we feel it is largely due to the new arrivals who are bringing their Mainland driving habits with them. Or maybe they tried for a while to do it the *Aloha* way and have just forgotten why they're here.

Road manners are a very small part of a big picture, but a part in which the results are clear and obvious. We just wish to encourage you to "practice *Aloha*" in your daily lives. If it is in your heart and it comes to you easily, it will become a way of life and you will be at peace here.

Be careful when selecting your place to call home. Be respectful of those whose lifestyles might differ from yours; they are your hosts here. When you find your special place, become a part of the community. Practicing *Aloha* means giving back to the community-giving of yourself. After a while, it becomes a fulfilling part of life here.

How you determine if this Island Paradise is really for you is entirely up to you. To those of us who make these magical Islands our home, Hawai'i is everything the name Paradise implies. We'd like it to be that way for you!

Wailoa Park, Hilo

Chapter Three

Finding Your Own Special Place

Hawai'i has long been famous for its high cost of living. The Big Island, however, has always been the exception and still is. Sure, there are very expensive homes and other properties here. If you wish, you can spend millions on a home. The good news is that if you're looking for a livable home to buy for $60,000, you can find that, too.

The Choices

The median house price here on the Hilo side of the Big Island, excluding the multi-million dollar properties, is around $120,000. In that range you have a lot of choices, like three- and four-bedroom homes, sometimes on an acre of lush tropical land. Some homes here have "*ohanas*." *Ohana* means family, and a real-estate listing showing an *ohana* has a second home on the property that was supposedly built for family, like maybe grandparents. These second homes are of course also useful as guest homes or even rentals, if the area is zoned to make that legal—and most are.

About now, you're probably thinking something like, "Wait a minute! How come all the statistics I've read say the median house price in Hawai'i is around $350,000?"

In your adventure through this book, you may notice that some of our claims seem optimistic when compared to the statistical reports you've read elsewhere. That's easy to explain. While we insist that it's easy to find an affordable lifestyle here on the Big Island, others will tell you that it still costs 30% more than a comparable lifestyle on the Mainland. They'll back up their claims of high costs of living with "the latest data pulled from all available sources." Well, yes, and from those sources, they're right.

Statistics: You've no doubt heard that old story about statistics: "Statistically, if you have one foot in the oven and the other on ice, you will be comfortable." Statistics can be—and regularly are—used to demonstrate nearly any claim. Sometimes this is done intentionally and other times it may be that this is the only way the researcher knows how to evaluate the situation.

Here's why a lot of available statistics are not viable tools in assessing the information you need. Hawai'i in general, and the Big Island in particular, has a unique set of demographics. Among them: the ratio of very expensive homes to very affordable homes is way different from "average Mainland" figures. In other words, average Mainland statistics will show a far smaller ratio of the total number of homes being in the super-expensive category than here in Hawai'i.

So yes, if you include all the million-dollar-and-up homes in your "Hawai'i home prices" average, that average will go way up. The problem with using these kinds of statistics when figuring Hawai'i's average home prices is that nobody who is seeking affordable homes here is even going to consider million-dollar homes. Or even $500,000 homes! So if you exclude all of the exceptions—the super-expensive homes of which there are many—the average home prices drop substantially. A quick look in the classifieds or in any of the free "homes & land" flyers and magazines (available free all over the Islands) will confirm the availability of a big selection of very affordable homes.

To many folks who are from the Mainland looking at homes here on the Big Island for the first time, the prices seem unbelievable. Actually, all of Hawai'i has been in a real estate down-market for about the last five years, but things are beginning to turn around. Now you'll see more new homes going up and the "for sale" signs coming down faster where a few years ago the market was all but dead. It's definitely still a good time to buy and Big Island prices are not likely to catch up with the other Islands at any time soon. At this point, the prices are climbing. Anything on the ocean or even with an ocean view has gone up dramatically in the last year, but the rest of the offerings are seeing more modest price increases.

As of this writing, California's high-tech community is finding Hawai'i to be well suited to their needs, and with the new companies moving here, willing employees are eagerly looking for housing. Home sales in the North Kona, South Kohala and Hamakua areas have been brisk in the last few months because of this activity.

Another influx we've noticed in our little beach community is that people nearing retirement age are buying homes while the prices are still down. Most plan to retire in anywhere from one to five years and they use their homes as rentals in the meanwhile. More on this in Chapter 8.

A Teaser

Here are some real estate ads from "Homes & Land," a free publication circulated here on the Island:

> Ocean view! One block to the ocean. Three bedrooms, two baths upstairs and one bedroom and one bath with a full kitchen downstairs. 1952 sq. ft. of living space, listed at $128,000.

Or how about this one:

> Three bedroom, three bath of 1567 sq. ft., on one acre! Lanai off of master bedroom, oak cabinets and Berber carpets. $169,000.

Still too much? Well then:

> Well cared-for home with fresh paint! Three bedrooms and two and a half baths on one acre with lots of grass. Birch cabinets and tile counter tops. Listed at $109,000.

Another one:

> Looking for a steal? This could be it! Well cared-for two bedroom home, 864 sq. ft. with screened-in lanai. Work shop or party room building in rear. $42,500.

Or how'd you like your own producing coffee farm?

> Coffee farm. 875 trees with redwood 3 bed 2.5 bath home on 1.87 acres. Must-sell price of $100,000. LH

The above ads are just a tiny smattering of what's available. There are big homes, tiny homes, income properties, farms, oceanfront homes, and bare land. You can also see the "Homes & Land" listings on their Web site at www.homes.com. Check the Resource Guide for more info.

To Buy or to Build

The way the prices are now, lots of homes are for sale at prices below what it would cost to replace them. If you find one that you happen to like, it would make no sense to build your own. The variety of properties is nearly endless, so there's a good chance you can find something that suits your needs.

This trend is slowly shifting, however, and in the more desirable areas where prices are starting to climb, it is once again worth considering building new. Among the benefits to think about in building new is the fact that wood has a finite lifespan here in the tropics and a new house won't need any immediate repairs for dryrot, termites and other humidity-related problems. And of course, you'll get to design the house you want instead of either settling for what's available or remodeling. An extensive remodel can actually cost as much as building a new house.

Not only is there a big variety in the homes available, but there's also a variety of climates, geographical features and flora. The Big Island has all but one of this planet's weather systems (Arctic), so you may choose from dense, low-elevation tropical forest where it's nearly always warm and humid; higher-elevation forest where it's cooler and drier; high-mountain desert with lots of dry grass and cactus (really!); right at the ocean's edge where it rains little and is always warm, or low-elevation leeward-side where it hardly rains at all.

Fee Simple, Leasehold and More

As you peruse the ads for homes in the two Big Island newspapers or any of the free "homes for sale" publications available all over the Island, you'll come across some terminology that might be confusing. Terms like Fee Simple, FEE, LH, HPP, HOVE and *ohana*. Let's take a quick look at those.

FS, Fee or Fee Simple means that the title to a property is clear and free from any leasehold encumbrances. The great majority of properties for sale on the Island are fee simple.

LH, or Leasehold, means that the building is owned free-and-clear but the land it sits upon is on a long-term lease. This doesn't really apply much any more, as most of the old leases have run out. There are still a few out there, especially on the Kona side, so we'll briefly explain. Since the few leases that are still in effect are likely to be near their expiration date, it is very important that you look at all the numbers. Many of the existing leases will show temptingly cheap annual or monthly payments, but be warned that when these leases come up for renegotiation, the lessors have routinely raised the rates by as much as 1000%. (That's one thousand—not a typo!)

Here's a typical example. We had a condo in Kailua-Kona, and the lease payments were an easy-to-manage $190 semi-annually. When the lease was close to its renegotiation date, the lessor sent out letters to the owners of each unit in the building. We now had the choice of continuing with the lease, with a new "adjusted" rate of $2,400 per year, or we could buy out the lessor's interest in that unit for $40,000. Not much of a choice, was it? We got lucky and sold the condo. The bottom line: If you get tempted by a low price on a LH property, make certain that you know the renegotiation date of the lease and whether the lessor has given out the new rates. If no new rates are available, you can use the above example as a guideline. It's fairly typical, according to the real-estate people we've talked to.

As a rule of thumb, you can figure that the cost of converting a leasehold property to a fee-simple property will be close to the difference between what the

LH property is worth and what a similar Fee-Simple property is worth. For example, if you find a LH one-bedroom, ocean-front condo for $70,000 and the very similar, Fee Simple, ocean-front, one-bedroom condos in the building down the street are selling for $110,000, the Fee-Simple conversion will probably cost about $40,000.

If you are looking at a property where the status of the title is not clearly shown, be sure to ask.

HPP is the common name (and the abbreviation) for Hawai'ian Paradise Park, a huge subdivision about ten miles south of Hilo. HOVE is Hawai'ian Ocean View Estates, an even more larger subdivision near the southernmost point of the Island. (These subdivisions are described in the Virtual Tour, Chapter 4.)

We cover *Ohana* elsewhere, but for this discussion it is simply the Hawai'ian word for family, and in the real-estate ad context it means that there is either an apartment or a second home on the property. Technically, a second "living unit" is any livable area, even a studio-sized apartment, that includes a kitchen. If the ad says "legal *ohana*," it means that the second living unit was permitted. If it doesn't say "legal," the second home or apartment may indeed have been legally built for family many years ago, but whether or not it could be used legally as a second home now is questionable. There are lots of these on the Island. Depending on what you would like to use the second home for, be sure to make any purchase offers conditional to the permitted use you intend.

Owner-built homes

You'll find quite a few owner-built homes here, and they can be either bargains or nightmares. A few of the considerations when looking over an owner-built home are whether or not the construction was done with a permit, whether or not the permit was ever signed off when the home was finished, and most importantly, the quality of the construction.

If a house was built with permits, you can at least be reasonably sure that the construction was up to code standards (at the time of construction). If there was no permit and you're still interested in the place, you need to look it over very carefully for construction and design flaws. If you aren't familiar with these concepts, you'd be way ahead to have somebody knowledgeable go with you to examine the structure.

Just because there was no permit is not, however, a good reason to reject a home! People do build without permits, especially in the more remote areas, and their workmanship often far surpasses that of most commercial builders. In this case, you might just score a bargain on the home because there are no permits, as that makes the place harder to sell.

One reason it's harder to sell a home with no permits is that it's difficult to get lenders to fund loans on unpermitted buildings. This is also why you'll see some very nice homes here with "seller financing" available. This can be a real bonus for the buyer, because seller financing involves a whole lot less red tape than going through a conventional lender, plus you don't need to qualify for the lenders' sometimes-way-to-strict rules.

Contrary to popular opinion, there are lenders who will fund loans on unpermitted buildings, though, so if you get a "no" from one, keep trying. The considerations here are how well the property appraises and the loan-to-value ratio. In other words, if you have a substantial down payment, you are far more likely to get a loan on an unpermitted building, or one that has an unpermitted addition or two. Be aware that some lenders will not only refuse a loan on anything unpermitted, but they will try to make you believe that this is standard policy among all lenders. Don't believe it.

Some lenders will loan only on the value of the permitted portion of the building. An example would be a home that was built with all the necessary permits but had a lanai added later with no permit. The appraiser will be instructed to appraise only the permitted portion of the home and to ignore the unpermitted lanai.

While we're talking about permits, another detail worth mentioning is that just because a building has been permitted and the permit has been signed off, is no guarantee that the building was built within the legal set-backs on the property. Strange as that might seem, it is a fact and this is one good reason to have a survey done on any property you get serious about. More on this later.

Seller financing is a bonus for self-employed folks, because they're in the group that is the least likely to be able to get conventional financing. Some sellers would rather have the monthly payments (and the interest!) than a lump sum of money to put into a savings account that pays almost no interest these days.

We occasionally hear from people trying to buy homes who tell us it's nearly impossible to get financing here unless you have a straight job and a sizable, dependable and documentable income. Not so. Several lenders and loan brokers here will finance just about anything as long as the numbers work. One in particular, has worked with us and others whom we know of and has been in business in the Islands for many years. Listed in the Resource Guide, this lender also makes "No-Doc" loans, meaning there is no requirement to show any income or financial statements. The loan is made strictly on the strength of your credit rating and the value-to-loan ratio. This is good for folks who, for example, want to buy an income property and know that their financial planning is sound and that the property will pay for itself, but can't get a conventional bank loan because they are self-employed or retired. If you would like options other than the one we list in the Resource Guide, ask your realtor for a lender who makes "no-doc" loans. And as with everything else in Hawaii, if your realtor looks at you as if you were nuts and says there is no such lender, just smile and say "Thank you!" and then go ask somebody else!

When house shopping, never let an asking price deter you from making a much lower offer. If you like the property and the price is out of your range, go ahead and offer what you would like to pay! You might just be surprised by the results. There's a big, two-story place near our home that was on the market for two years with an asking price of $120,000. It finally sold for $70,000. It needed some repairs, for sure, but it was a nice looking home, about 200 feet from the ocean, and the new owner has brought the value way up with very little money and a month or two of work.

Unfortunately, this worked a lot better a year or two ago than it does now. Today, most fairly-priced homes in good locations sell at their asking prices. If you're looking for a real deal, seek out the exception: a real junker (but with terrific possibilities) in a good neighborhood, or the very nice owner-built-without-permits home that is hard to sell because a bank won't loan on it. Ask your realtor to give you a list of homes that have been on the market for a month or more. Also, try to find one realtor who you can work with and who will be your representative as the buyer.

If you're working with an owner-seller (rather than with a realtor), be sure to ask for a disclosure statement, and then have a title company do the paperwork for you. It doesn't cost that much, and it is a lot safer than buying real estate with a simple contract between buyer and seller. Often a deal goes through smooth as silk, but sometimes there are glitches that the title company will catch with their routine procedure that could become major hassles down the road if left undetected. This is especially important with rural properties as opposed to those in subdivisions, but it even applies there.

We recently sold a home in an established subdivision only to discover that the buyer's survey disclosed that the house was built into the setback! (A "setback" is the distance a building is required to be "set back" from a property line. Setbacks vary from location to location and differ between front, side and rear property lines.) We did not do a survey when we bought this house because the seller was a realtor as well as a builder and we made some invalid assumptions!

You have two options when it comes to finding the true boundaries of the property you're looking to buy. One is a full survey, which can get expensive. The other is to hire a "pin finder" to find the existing property pins (the permanent corner markers of the property, put there by a previous survey). If you are looking at a rural property, especially one that has irregular boundaries, you should definitely order a survey. In most sales through realtors, this is required anyway, and the seller usually pays for it.

Here's an example of why a survey is more thorough than a simple pin location. We recently bought a little house to use as a vacation rental. Had we hired a pin finder, he would have found the pins that were clearly visible at what appeared to be the lot corners, and that would have been the extent of his responsibility. A survey, however, brought a crew who had the latest Platt map which clearly showed a conflict between the pin locations and where the lot lines should have been. It turns out that the previous owner of this property and the adjacent lot had had the boundary line moved several years ago. The reason was that he had intended to build his home on the adjacent lot and the boundary-line move gave him an extra ten feet by taking the ten feet from the lot our little house was on. The surveyors, with some extra diligence, found an additional and barely-visible set of pins defining the new lot line. Had we relied on a pin finder, this sale would have gone on record with the wrong lot dimensions.

Simply having the wrong lot dimensions recorded with the sale of the house would not be a big deal in itself, but what if we would have decided to add onto the house and build that addition right up to the setback of that incorrect property line? The building department most likely would not have caught the error when they issued us a building permit, but maybe the adjacent lot owner would have complained about the intrusion onto his property, which could conceivably start a long, drawn out legal procedure and even force the removal of the addition.

One trick worth mentioning is that if you are considering a subdivision property and no survey is required in the purchase but you would like to know where the property lines are, look at the adjacent several lots to see if there has been a recent survey done. You're looking for a stake with a colored ribbon tied to it, or a pipe driven into the ground. If you find pins on an adjacent lot, you can find the pins on your lot by carefully measuring from the existing pins. Of course you will need a plot plan with measurements, or even a plot map of the area, some of which have lot measurements. If there's no plot plan available, use the dimensions on the realtor's listing agreement. Measure the lot on which you found the pins, and if it is of the same dimensions as those shown for your lot, it is reasonably safe to assume that all of the lots are the same size. "Reasonably safe," by the way, means it's OK to use this method to find lot boundaries when you're looking at a property, but it is not safe enough to rely on as the last word in the final purchase.

It's best to do what you can to be sure of your boundaries.

In Hawai'i it's also smart to ask for a termite report, and if you don't feel competent to make a thorough inspection of the property yourself, hire a home inspector to do it for you. Again, hiring a Title and Escrow service to do the paperwork for you will make sure that all bases are covered. Even if you can handle real-estate transactions on your own, there's high probability that Hawai'i requires documents or procedures that your home state did not, and it is best for all parties concerned to do it right the first time. The cost is insignificant in the big picture. See the Resource Guide for a recommendation.

It is also important to know that dryrot is a bigger problem in many areas that termite damage, and a termite inspection generally ignores dryrot. The report will mention only termite (or other insect) damage. Again, if you do not feel qualified to do these inspections yourself, please hire a competent home inspector. We have listed one with whom we are familiar in the Resource Guide.

Free Information

Once you find a house or piece of land you're interested in, it could be to your advantage to know some history about it. The tax office in Hilo will let you use their computer to look up any piece of real estate.

All you need to know is the Tax Map Key, or "TMK." This is the number that identifies that particular parcel of land exactly, and it will be on any listing agreement or form that you get from realtors describing a property they are showing you. If that isn't available and it's important to you to look up the info, you can consult the area maps available at the public library and find the TMK yourself. Most realtors also have these TMK maps in their offices and will let you look up a specific parcel. When you're still at the property, make note of any landmarks at or near the lot in question, like how many lots from the corner of what streets. That will make it easier for you to locate the correct parcel on the map.

The public documents at the tax office consist of a history of current and previous owners, a description of the parcel, what its land and structure assessments are and have been over the years, any sales and the dollar amounts of those sales. The amount and date of the last sale of a parcel can be valuable bargaining information for you when buying a place.

If a parcel or home has been sold every few years over the last ten, it would be a good idea to find out why. If the current owner has only had it for a year or less, why is it being sold again? If the current owner recently bought it for half of what he's trying to sell it for now, is he in the business of buying and selling for profit? These and other considerations can all be of use when coming up with an offer. See the Resource Guide for the addresses and phone numbers of the Hilo Office and the Library.

In Conclusion . . .

Don't listen to all those "statistical reports" on how expensive it is to live in Hawai'i! Check it out for yourself, and you will be pleasantly surprised. You can do a lot of preliminary checking on the many Hawai'i real-estate Web sites. Just type "Hawai'i real estate" into your browser and click your way to the Big Island. Check the Resource Guide for some specific Web addresses.

We mentioned before to try finding a realtor with whom you can enjoy working and who will be your representative as the buyer. Remember, if you go to the listing realtor, s/he is the *seller's* representative and has the seller's best interests in mind at all times. It is clearly to your advantage to use the services of a realtor who has *your* best interests in mind!

On The Big Island, you can find anything from a grass shack to a fantastic ocean-front home; any kind of climate from desert-dry to rain-forest; you can be in town or as rural as you like; live in a subdivision lot or have your very own farm. And the best part is that it's all affordable!

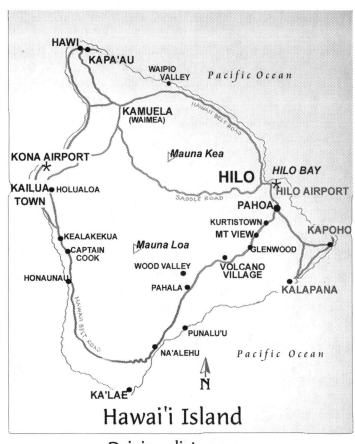

Hawai'i Island

Driving distances

Hilo to Kailua Town by way of Kamuela: 100 miles
Hilo to Kamuela: 59 miles
Kailua Town to Na'alehu: 57 miles
Hilo to Na'alehu: 55 miles
Kamuela to Hawi: 21 miles

Chapter Four

The Virtual Island Tour

N ow let's take a tour of the entire Island. We'll stop in each community and take a good look around, so you'll have a basic idea of what to expect. With this information you should be able to narrow your search to a few possibilities instead of spending weeks on an actual tour. At the very least, you'll be able to eliminate places that get really cold if you like to stay warm, homes up in the mountains if beaches are important to you, or places that are an hour's drive from town if you'll need to commute.

Our itinerary starts in Hilo and goes around the Island in a clockwise direction (assuming you're looking at a map).

This will be our around-the-Island itinerary. The indented names are subdivisions and small communities.

Hilo
Kea'au
      HPP
      Orchidland
      Ainaloa
      Hawai'ian Beaches

Hawai'ian Parks
Hawai'ian Shores
Nanawale
Pahoa
Kapoho
Leilani Estates
Red Road area
Kehena Beach Estates
Kalapana Seaview
Puna Palisades
Kurtistown
Mountain View
Glenwood
Fern Forest Estates
Fern Acres (a.k.a. Crescent Acres)
Hawai'ian Acres
Volcano
Wood Valley
Pahala
Na'alehu
HOVE (Hawai'an Ocean View Estates)
Honaunau
Captain Cook
Kealakekua
Holualoa
Kailua-Kona
Subdivisions close-in to Kailua Village
Subdivisions north (toward airport) of Kailua Village
Kawaihae
Hawi
Kapa'au

Waimea (Kamuela)
Honoka'a
Laupahoehoe
Honomu
Papa'ikoa
Back to Hilo

The Virtual Tour

Our tour begins and ends in Hilo. We'll cover each stop on the tour with a general description of the community, the weather, the ambiance, and any noteworthy things you need to know. If any of the places we visit have special reputations, such as beauty, safety, serenity, or even crime, we'll let you know.

Let's look at some factors common to many of the areas so we won't have to repeat the same info for each place. First, the terms "*mauka*" and "*makai*." In Hawai'i, we use a unique system to describe direction. Since all the Islands are basically round(ish) and the main roads go around the outside of the Islands, the usual terms of north, south, east and west are difficult to apply here. So we use *mauka* and *makai*.

Mauka means toward the mountain. You can remember it by the phonetic association of *mauka* and MAUntain. *Makai* means toward the ocean. *Kai* is the Hawai'ian word for ocean. Actually, anywhere you find yourself, it's almost always easy to tell which way is *mauka* and which is *makai*. Usually, *mauka* is the uphill direction and *makai* is the downhill direction. After a while, it becomes quite natural and you always know where the ocean is relative to where you are at the time.

Another term you'll see on our tour is "catchment system." Many of the homes here, even those in large developments, rely on rainwater catchment systems for their domestic water needs. On the Windward (Hilo) side of the Island, this works well because there is usually enough rain to keep the system well supplied. These systems consist of a metal roof on the house, rain gutters with pipes directing the water into a large (usually 6-10,000 gallon) tank, and then a pressure tank and pump just like on a system that uses a well. Properly designed and constructed catchment systems are very reliable and the water, usually run through one or more filters, is great. It's soft, mineral-free and tastes wonderful. Some people don't drink their catchment water, but most do. We have for years and prefer it by a wide margin to any municipal water we've ever tasted.

Some of the homes in remote areas have solar electrical systems, too. There are whole subdivisions that have only recently had municipal power run in, and with much controversy at that. A lot of the people who had well-working solar systems didn't want the ugly utility poles and wires in their views, while others who had inefficient or substandard systems welcomed the utility into the neighborhood. The power company fought hard to preserve their "right" to install their poles and wires anywhere they wanted to, and as usual, the big guys won.

One last thing before we begin our tour. As you drive through the communities of the Big Island, you might wonder why so many homes appear to be built up on stilts. The reason is to catch breezes! Especially if the home is in a forest, or even if there are trees or shrubs around that would block the prevailing tradewinds from the building, a house built on stilts will be much cooler and more comfortable inside when it's up high enough that the breezes come through. It's as simple as that. When you see houses near the ocean built way up high, it's because of the new building regulations requiring any home within range of high-tide or winter-storm ocean waves to be built that high. Some of them seem really ridiculous built as high as they are, especially when they're right between two other homes built right on the ground. The two other ones were built before the experts decided on the new rules, and some of them have survived 50 or more years of winter storms without ever getting wet. Go figure.

OK, here we go! Our first stop will be the beautiful city of Hilo.

Hilo

Hilo is our favorite little city in the world. Hilo is, to us, the essence of *Aloha*! The people are gentle and friendly, and life moves at a pace that's comfortable and easy-going. Hilo is rich in the heritage of these islands, and it shows in daily life here as well as in the varied and frequent cultural events.

Hilo is a city of parks. The highway running along the edge of beautiful Hilo Bay is lined with parks on both sides. Often, you'll see kids' soccer games or other sports activities going on there, and there are picnic areas and even a pavilion in which you can enjoy all sorts of musical events. Along the waterfront at Hilo

Bay are canoe sheds filled with the exotic craft used by canoe clubs and cultural events.

Liliuokalani Gardens is a formal Japanese garden park off of scenic Banyan Drive. There are small bridges over quiet ponds, pagodas, stone lanterns, and an ambiance that is distinctly inviting. Nearby is Coconut Island, yet another park and this one is accessible by footbridge. This small island is the home to some unique Hawai'ian cultural events and is commonly used for weddings and other gatherings. The cover photo on this book was taken from Coconut Island. All of these places provide a very relaxing atmosphere for a day's meandering.

Liliuokalani Gardens on the Hilo waterfront

Banyan Drive is where most of Hilo's hotels are located, and the drive is worthwhile even if you're not looking for lodging! Alongside the curving road are huge banyan trees, planted many years ago by celebrities like Richard Nixon, Amelia Earhart, and others. Their names appear on plaques at the foot of each tree. At one end of the drive is an inlet from the Bay where many small sailing boats are moored. There's a white sand beach there, too, and hardly ever more than a few people!

If you're not yet tired of parks, drive out Kalanianaole Avenue about four miles to the end, and all along that ride you'll see the most inviting small parks on the ocean side of the road. In many, you'll see children playing in the shallow, crystal-clear tide-pools, while the older and more adventuresome are out playing in the surf beyond. Picnic areas, pavilions and other park facilities seem to be everywhere along this beautiful drive. Near the end of the road is Richardson Beach Park, and here it's definitely worth your while to get out of your car and take a walk. The ocean vistas are awesome, and the park itself is friendly and beautiful. The accessibility of all these wonderful places is just another reason why Hilo is a great place to live.

If this is starting to sound like a travel-guide sponsored by the Hilo Chamber of Commerce, it's only because of our never-ending enthusiasm for our favorite little city.

Hilo is home to the Hilo Campus of the University of Hawai'i and Hawai'i Junior College. The University Theater presents all sorts of incredible performances throughout the year. The newly-restored Palace Theater in the Old Downtown area also features old movies and art films as well as stage plays and cultural events. There are several fine art galleries, and all sorts of outlets for every conceivable kind of artistic endeavor.

Our little City is also home to some exceptional dining establishments, some of which feature live music most nights. And of course the hotels have regular dining extravaganzas, complete with Hawai'ian (and sometimes Tahitian) music and dance performances. Although these are intended for the tourist trade, a lot of us who live here occasionally take advantage of the fun and food, too.

A portion of the Hilo Campus, University of Hawai'i

For those who are dedicated shoppers, Hilo features the only genuine mall on the Island. Just about anything you could ever need is available somewhere in town, and it has been our experience that prices are not much higher than what you'd pay on the Mainland-

providing you are willing to shop around. (See Chapter 6, "Shopping.")

There is a gentle, almost turn-of-the-century quality to Hilo. The Old Downtown area is being slowly restored as funds become available and is looking better every year. There are old stores that will bring back warm, nostalgic feelings to many, and right along with them are coffee houses where you can go enjoy an excellent espresso. There are mom-and-pop stores that have been in the same families for generations, and lots of new small businesses, too.

Hilo is a city of variety. It's a place where families live, work and raise their children. It really is unlike any other city or town in Hawai'i, in that the few tourists who mingle in with the residents are just people who seem to fit in, as opposed to some of the heavily touristed places where the tourist crush seems to be overwhelming at times. Nobody seems to be in a hurry in Hilo; everybody has time to be courteous and thoughtful.

The nights in Hilo are wonderful, too. The air is sweet and warm, the lights are soft and gentle, and the pace is even slower than during the day. Once each year, Hilo has it's annual Ho'olau'lea (party), where several blocks of the Old Downtown area are closed to traffic and there's just one big, gala street party! About a dozen live bands share the three music stages and play long into the night, food booths line the streets for blocks, and a few thousand happy people are walking, talking, and dancing the night away. There's even one of those old-timey giant searchlights with a beam that pierces the sky, like some theaters had back in the olden days. Are you old enough to remember those?

Hilo is the business center of this side of the Island and also the County Seat for Hawai'i County (all of the Big Island). For this reason, it's also where many of the regular jobs are found.

Hilo's "Old Town"

The residential areas of Hilo vary a lot in many ways. Most are clean and tidy, but that's where the similarity ends. Some are new developments of fancy homes in the $200,000-up category, others are tracts of larger acreages with homes in about the same range and higher, and then there are the many older, established areas in which home sizes, styles, ages and quality vary so much that the prices go from under $100,000 to over

$600,000. There are always beautiful homes available in Hilo for between $100,000 and $200,000.

The size and scope of Hilo's residential areas is hard to visualize from just driving around town. You can get a better idea by taking the roads going *mauka*, so you can oversee the city from the hills. Also, take a look at the map of Hilo in the front of the phone book. It's an excellent street guide, too.

A view from the hills of Hilo

On your inter-Island flight from Honolulu to Hilo, get a window seat as far forward as you can and on the right side of the airplane. From this vantage point, you'll get a great view of the entire city, including the residential areas that extend up into the hills. You'll also get to view the Hamakua Coast all the way down into

Hilo, and that will give you an idea of the many residential areas along the ocean.

One recent turn of events is that the University has experienced a huge increase in enrollment in the last year, and of course, this is having an effect on the availability of housing in the area. And as usual, when the supply goes down, the price goes up. While the effect is most obvious on rentals, it will carry over to home sales, as well.

Hilo has the reputation of being the rainiest city on earth. Clearly, this has not been our experience. More often than not, our weekly (and sometimes more often) trips to Hilo find our favorite city in brilliant sunshine. Our own experiences aside, it does rain a lot in Hilo and you should know that the amount of rain, like in every other place on the Island, varies a great deal with minor differences in elevation. As soon as you leave sea-level and drive up into the hills, you'll be heading into more frequent rain. The Kaumana area of Hilo is absolutely beautiful, featuring many homes with breathtaking views, but its higher elevation makes it famous for rain.

In all fairness, we have to admit that a once in a while, even after all these years, we forget the Rule of Parking: roll up your windows! (If you drive a convertible, put the top up!) Our car for years was a convertible, and sometimes we'd pull up to the grocery store on a gorgeous, sunny day, go in for some shopping, and upon our return to the car it's still sunny but the inside of the car is soaked! What happened? A squall came through. This is the kind of rain we've experienced in Hilo the most; the occasional rain-squall during a sunny day. Even though you get a little wet, it's still nice and warm and you dry right off again. Think of it as refreshing.

"All this rain" is a subjective thing, too. For example, if you're moving here from Seattle, there are two distinct differences. One thing you'd notice right away is that even when it's raining, it's still warm outside. The other is that instead of a constant drizzle as you would experience in Seattle, we get our rain all at once! Hilo might get the same amount of rain as Seattle during a particular day, but Hilo gets it all in ten minutes. And then it mostly rains at night. Now on the other hand, if your last home was in Arizona, the rain might be a bit much for you. One thing you'll find here is that the folks who live here and love it don't even notice the rain. It's all part of the beauty of the Windward side. And indeed, after one of our occasional overnighters to the Kona side, we always appreciate the refreshing rain when we come back home.

The bottom line: If the thought of a home, perhaps even a gracious older home in excellent condition with a sweeping view of the city and the beautiful Hilo Bay gets you going, look around in Hilo. There are homes like that available, and the prices will never be better.

Kea'au

Moving right along, just six miles south, toward the town of Volcano on Highway 11 (*mauka* on the Volcano Highway), we come to Kea'au. Kea'au seems like little more than a small shopping center to folks traveling through. Matter of fact, a recent new highway project called the Kea'au Bypass means that now you can go from Hilo to the Lower Puna (Pahoa, Kapoho, Kalapana) area without even going through Kea'au any more at all.

Kea'au is a small, pleasant community of homes mostly situated on the *makai* side of the highway. Exploring the side roads of the area will bring you to a lot of the "private property" signs on the entries to mill and other lands closed to the public. One of the most beautiful beaches on this side of the Island is at the end of one of these private roads and is accessible to the public only by a long and difficult walk along the rocky coastline. Too bad about that.

Also included in the Kea'au area are many small farms and other rural properties not right within the community. Kea'au weather is not unlike Hilo, except that the slightly higher elevation makes it a little wetter and cooler.

Kea'au will also shortly be the site of a new multi-million-dollar shopping center to go along with the big new residential tracts proposed for the immediate area. One thing Kea'au does not need is a big shopping center right outside the village. This will be the final nail in the coffin for all of the small businesses in the community. Unfortunately, the big guys who build multi-million-dollar shopping centers do not much care about the impact their projects have on the existing business community. The shops in Hilo will also suffer as a result of this project, and the increased traffic at the already busy Kea'au intersections will become the problem of those who must commute through this corridor. Too bad about that.

Hawai'ian Paradise Park (HPP)

On the highway from Kea'au to Pahoa (Hwy 130), this enormous residential development, also known as "HPP" or "Paradise Park," contains thousands of one-acre lots and hundreds of homes. Land and home prices are reasonable here, ranging from well under $100,000 for decent homes to over twice that amount for nice ones near the ocean.

A typical Farmer's Market

The ocean frontage of this development affords some fantastic views, but there is no ocean access because the whole coastline in the area is a cliff that averages around twenty feet high.

With the exception of the main roads from the highway all the way to the ocean (a distance of about five miles), all of the intersecting roads are unpaved.

There are no water or sewer lines, so each home has its own water catchment and septic systems. HPP is what we like to refer to as "spotty," meaning there are beautiful homes right alongside humble ones. Same goes for the terrain. A lot of HPP looks barren and dry, while the edges of the development and the parts down near the ocean are wooded and attractive.

HPP is just 15 minutes from Hilo, so it's a desired location for many people who work in town. In Hawai'i, long commutes are unheard of and highly undesirable by most people. HPP lots and homes cost more than those in nicer areas farther out simply because of their close proximity to town. The weather in HPP is about the same as in Hilo, but it also varies within the community. As in most areas on the Island, the closer you get to the ocean, the drier the climate. The elevation climb as you go *mauka* brings more rain.

Orchidland

Who dreamed up these names, anyway? Were they running a "corny contest" at the time? OK, Orchidland, right across Highway 130 from HPP, is another large tract of lots with homes on only a small percentage of them. Again, the streets are unimproved, and in dry weather, very dusty. Homes in this development tend to be of less value than in nearby HPP. Orchidland relies on catchment water systems and individual septic systems.

Ainaloa, Hawai'ian Beaches, Hawai'ian Shores, Nanawale, and others

We'll group these together because of their similarity in many ways. They are all medium-size tracts (by East Hawai'i standards) with only part of the lots having homes on them. Nanawale is more densely populated than the other two, and the lots there are small. The prices in all are near the bottom for homes. There is a larger percentage of month-to-month rentals in these developments, and the general ambiance is not as well-kept as in other communities nearby. For some reason, there is also a disproportionally-high crime rate here, mostly small-time burglaries, and some domestic violence and drug-related incidents. Most of these tracts are on catchment water systems and individual septic systems.

"Hawai'ian Shores" is the community on the right side of the main road going down into the "Hawai'ian Beaches" area and is clearly the exception to some of the above. It is a private subdivision with an Association and some rules that make for a more pleasant community. There are far fewer rentals here, and there's a private water system, eliminating the need for catchment tanks.

Again, weather depends on elevation. The closer to the ocean, the warmer and dryer it is.

Life in the community of Nanawale has improved a lot in the last year or two because of a well-run neighborhood watch program that has a lot of support from the community. The basic philosophy of the programs is that the thieves generally cruise a neighborhood before attempting any of their mischief. If they see the occasional car with a "Neighborhood Watch Patrol" magnetic sign on the side, they know that this isn't going to be easy and they go elsewhere. It sounds to simple, perhaps, but we've seen it work in several communities now.

The really effective programs are the ones with enthusiastic community support. There will be a "phone tree," so that if somebody needs assistance or is observing something suspicious going on, there's always a neighbor close by who will respond. A potential thief who knows he is being watched is going to think twice about doing a burglary; if a neighbor shows up also sporting the "Patrol" signs on his car, the thief is out of there for good. It's all about neighbors helping neighbors.

Pahoa

About 11 miles from Kea'au and past the HPP and Orchidland subdivisions we come to Pahoa, the historic little village that time seems to have forgotten. The 100-year-old buildings and wooden sidewalks are basically unchanged over the years, although you will see newer structures here and there. In sharp contrast to the old ambiance is the new, state-of-the-art, Olympic-size swimming pool facility. Some state-wide swim meets are held here occasionally, and other than that, the pool gets little use. Perhaps it's because most of the kids here would rather play in the ocean than in a pool? It is open to the public for free daily use. The pool is located near the Community Center right in the middle of the village.

You can make a day of just people-watching in Pahoa! Pahoa is reminiscent of a 60's-era small town in Northern California, with its colorful characters and old-west ambiance. There are all sorts of interesting places: excellent restaurants featuring Mexican, Chinese, Italian, BBQ, vegetarian, Thai, local-style and ordinary American-style; gift and curio shops; imported clothing; two grocery stores and a brand-new natural-foods store. There's a gas station, post office, two banks, a 7-11, and excellent hardware store and of course, a pawn shop.

Main Street, Pahoa Town

Pahoa is the service center for a much larger geographical area than just the tiny town, as is evidenced by the huge K-12 school campus and the 1000-kid enrollment there.

Except for a very small area of ancient, colorful and quaint homes on the few side streets in the village, Pahoa includes very little actual residential area. There are many rural homes nearby, and the rest of the population that frequents Pahoa lives in the surrounding large tracts of homes. These include Nanawale, Leilani Estates and a few not-so-nearby: Kehena Beach Estates, Kalapana Seaview, Puna Palisades and others. These last few are all down near the end of Highway 130, about ten miles from Pahoa.

Highway 130 used to go all the way around the Island, but the lava flows of the early 90s covered enough of the road that it will probably never be rebuilt. If you like this area and would like to see some of the non-tract homes for sale, ask your realtor to find the listings for you. We've found some very interesting places this way that we would never have come across on our own. Among them are small farms and very rural homes on small acreages upslope behind the town. The road that accesses this area goes up through the middle of the high-school campus.

Kapoho

Now we're going to take a small detour and head *makai* from Pahoa on Highway 132 to Kapoho. Kapoho has the reputation of being the sunniest spot on the windward side of the Island, and indeed it seems to be. The three small communities in Kapoho enjoy the creatively inspired names of Beach Lots, Farm Lots and (get this!) Vacationland.

Beach Lots is the most expensive part and has some beautiful homes, fantastic ocean frontage and easy ocean access. There are calm lagoons right in some of the yards, and perfect for snorkeling or just playing in the water. Some are even heated for you by Mother Nature's geothermal springs. Homes for sale are rare, and when they come on the market they sell for a minimum of $200,000 up to well over $600,000. Hardly "affordable." With some notable exceptions, most of the homes are on small lots, as is the case with most ocean-front property. The bigger parcels of land are very pricey. But don't despair; if you really take a liking to Beach Lots, you can still occasionally find small, older homes needing upgrading in this gated oceanfront community for a manageable price. When it happens, it doesn't take long for the house to sell, so you have to stay on top of the market here. The whole Kapoho area has been, as they say, discovered, and much of it is being bought up by folks who use their purchases as vacation rentals until the time that they can retire there.

The Farm Lots area is comprised of five-acre lots zoned as farm land, or in zoning-speak, "AG" for agriculture. Many of these have been bought for that purpose and most of those are orchid farms with the owners' homes on the property. Some get bought by folks with no farming intentions but who just want more privacy. The lots are currently going for $60-75,000. The terrain varies from flat to sloping, and the vegetation is heavy on some lots and sparse on others. Since there are already quite a few established flower farms in this area, you need to know that there is chemical spraying going on. If you get interested in a place in the Farm Lots, it's a good idea to make sure it is upwind from any flower farms or possible future flower farms. The reason is that if you are downwind, you'll be in the wind path of all the spraying. Basically, this means finding a lot on the ocean side of the subdivision.

A Hawai'i sunset   Photo: Camille Thomsen

And last but not least, we come to Vacationland, a curious little community of homes ranging from big and expensive to tiny but not cheap. A few years ago, it was hard to give away a home here. Now it's hard to keep one on the market for more than a few weeks. A two-bedroom house on one of the 8,000 square-foot lots can go for as little as $100,000, and a big, two-story home with a fantastic tidal pond in the back yard just sold for $285,000. Tiny ocean-front cabins have been bringing $140,000 and up, but the homes a few blocks from the beach are still reasonable. Vacationland has had a reputation as a kind of rough place, and to a degree it still is. There is a notorious group of about eight homes right in the center of the community, all owned by the same person and all rented to folks who don't seem to have a lot of pride in their environs. The evidence is the obvious lack of maintenance of homes and yards and in some cases, the colorful bed-sheets used as curtains. But it's easy to avoid this little area and the rest of the community is nice. Not fancy or the least bit upscale, but nice.

There are new homes being built in Vacationland, and our feeling is that it won't be long before the whole community is cleaned up. Building new seems to be the best way to go right now, because the lot prices are still comparably low. Nice ones not on the ocean are selling for $20-30,000.

The location of this little community is awesome, and has a fantastic ocean access with calm, tide pools and reef-protected swimming and snorkeling. The marine-life and coral formations are unique to this area and bring lots of weekend visitors, making the ocean access area crowded on those days. There is talk in the community of installing a gate like at Beach Lots to keep the vehicle traffic down to those who live there. All three of these Kapoho communities have County water available, but not all the homes are hooked up. New hookups run from $6,000 and up. For this reason, many homes are still on catchment systems, and all are on private septic systems.

Leilani Estates

Here is where you'll find one of the best values in homes! The catch, and we'll expose it right up front, is most of Leilani is too rainy for a lot of people. That said, Leilani is one of the most beautiful, well-kept and safest communities on the Island. It consists of about 2,000 one-acre lots, most of them over 400 feet deep. The depth of the lots prompts most residents to build far back on their property, giving the community a unique look. Many of the homes cannot be seen from the roads. All you see is an inviting curvy driveway heading back through lush, green forest and dazzling flowers. There are some pretty basic homes in Leilani, and there are some very special ones as well. In only the very top few streets of Leilani Estates, the roads are unpaved and this small area is not covered by Leilani's Owners Association minimal rules or restrictions. In this small area of Leilani, you can find homes at unbelievable prices. A friend bought a livable two-bedroom home there a year ago for $14,500, and we've seen some pretty nice ones go for under $50,000!

Prices for decent homes in the main subdivision range from around $80,000 to over $200,000. You can buy a very nice 1500 sq. ft. home with a 2-car garage in the $100-135,000 range in Leilani, and lots vary from $6,000 to $12,000 for all but the few (distant) ocean-view parcels, and they bring $25,000 and up.

Strange as it might seem, the cost of homes in Leilani is also kept down by the 35 minute drive to Hilo. Folks here just don't do mainland-style commutes.

When we lived in Leilani, I would occasionally advertise a car for sale in the paper. Somebody would call from Hilo and when he found out I lived in Leilani he'd get mad at me. "I don't drive that far to take my family on vacation," he'd tell me and then hang up. The way we look at it is the drive to Hilo (or anywhere else on the Island, for that matter) is so beautiful and the traffic is never a problem, so why not just enjoy it?

Back to the rain part, Leilani varies about 400 feet in elevation from the upper portion to the lower end, and the upper part, at about 1000 feet in elevation, is the rainiest. It's obvious when you drive through, that the upper part, nearest the highway, is a lush, dense rain forest, and as the name implies, it takes a lot of moisture to keep it green. The forest becomes more sparse as the elevation drops, and just that little change in elevation is enough to make a significant difference in the rainfall.

When we lived there, we were closer to the bottom than to the top, and sometimes we'd be on the phone with a friend who lived nearer the top and he'd talk of how hard it was raining while it was sunny at our house. The cooler elevation of Leilani is preferred by some folks because the temps usually run about 10 degrees less on any given day than at sea level. The rule-of-thumb is that the temp drops about ten degrees per thousand feet elevation. Of course there are exceptions, but that's why it's called a rule-of-thumb!

Leilani has had a very effective "neighborhood watch" program going on for some years now, and because of it, it's one of the safest subdivisions on the Island. During our seven years there, we seldom locked anything. We left the keys in our cars and the house was nearly always open.

Leilani is also a very well maintained community. The roadsides are kept neatly mowed, which is a major job, what with the many miles of road and the rate of growth of everything! The pavement is kept in good repair and the whole subdivision has a nice feel to it when driving through. The deep lots mean that there will almost never be a car parked on the street, which in itself gives a different kind of feeling.

A house-hunting tip for anywhere on the Island: Take note of the vegetation around you. If you're in a lush rain forest, even if it happens to be a sunny and bright day, please believe that it rains a lot there. That's why it's a rain forest. We heard from a few folks who bought in Leilani during some great, sunny weather only to be disappointed later when they saw how much it rained there. Again, a lot of rain to one person is just the right amount to another. Some folks would rather it never rained and others couldn't live without it. Best you feel it for yourself. One other thing to watch for in Leilani, as in any other place here that gets a lot of rain is evidence of mildew. Mildew can be a real problem in some places, and it's usually evident as black, sooty-looking deposits on exterior walls, rafters and any other places outside that don't get a lot of air flow or sunlight. Inside, mildew is often first noticed by its smell. The odor bothers some folks a lot and others not at all. Interior mildew can be found in dark places like closets and even on walls behind doors that are seldom closed. Don't forget to look up, too, as it likes to accumulate on ceilings in rooms with little air flow or sunlight.

Kalapana and Vicinity

From Pahoa, we head down Highway 130 (called the Pahoa-Kalapana Highway) to Kalapana. Kalapana was once the site of the famous Kalapana Black Sand Beach, which sadly got covered with a thick, wide layer of lava in the early 90s. There are rural homes (homes not in communities and possibly on larger lots than are normally found in tracts) and even some small communities off of this highway between Pahoa and Kalapana, and if you're into seclusion, you can find some bargains here. Whenever you see a home listed for sale for $40,000, it's likely you'll find it in this area. Some of these small subdivisions are run-down, have substandard owner-built houses and reputations that are less than inviting, so be careful and look closely. As you peruse the offerings, let your intuition be your guide.

Kehena Beach Estates

Where Highway 130 dead-ends into Highway 137 (the Red Road), we'll take a left. Now we're driving through some dry, scrubby terrain, and in a couple of miles we come to a sudden change of scenery: a lush tropical forest! Just into the forest is the little community of Kehena Beach Estates, or more commonly, just Kehena. This is an area of small lots with homes that range from tiny to huge, from humble to finely-crafted, and in prices from $70,000 to over $300,000. Some of the pricey offerings are on more than one lot. It's a friendly community of folks from all walks of life, some young, some old, mostly self-employed or not working straight jobs for one reason or another.

One of the big attractions of living here is Kehena Beach, a gorgeous little black sand beach only a short walk from anywhere in the community. The beach itself is down a short-but-steep trail, and when you get down there you're in another world. The beach is small, only about 300 feet long. It's a crescent of shimmering black sand nestled into a 30-foot-high cliff, with palms and all sorts of tropical growth adding to the primeval ambiance. This is a clothing-optional beach, but it's also very much a family place, where on any given day you'll see kids from 2 to 82 playing in the surf, enjoying the warm sun, and in a climate of peace and quiet. Some people are clothed, others are not, and nobody seems to care. Often there will be somebody gently strumming a guitar or maybe even the strains of a flute coming from somewhere in the distance.

On many mornings, you can watch pods of spinner dolphins frolicking close enough to the shore that people will swim out to play with them. It really is a special place.

Kehena recently got electric lines run in but a number of homes are still on solar systems. The community relies on catchment water and individual septic systems. The weather here is usually clear and sunny, even when it's raining elsewhere close by. Kehena is a special place for special people. It's not one of those middle-of-the-road communities; you'll either love it or it won't do a thing for you.

Kalapana Seaview and Puna Palisades

Both of these tracts are walking distance to Kehena Beach (see above description) and both have ocean-view parcels and homes. Both are sparsely populated at this point, but there is definite building activity going on. Palisades (another of those inspired names) feels much better to us, in that it's smaller and the homes are of a more consistent quality. Among nicer homes, Seaview has some that you have to wonder how they withstand a good breeze without collapsing. Both communities have electric power but no water or sewers. Catchment systems are the norm for domestic water. The power came in recently, so there are still homes there on solar systems, and most of them are substandard at best. Beware when looking at a home that the owner says is "on solar." If you have no experience with this sort of thing but are open to looking into it, be sure to have the home checked out by a solar contractor before you get real serious. Probably all you need do is take a list of the major components to any solar contractor to find out if the system can be expected to support the house. Most cannot, and the owners run noisy little generators to supplement their power needs.

Prices in Palisades are higher than Seaview, but even so, when homes come on the market there, fairly decent ones go for around $120,000. Again, sunshine is the order of the day here. Both communities are barren when compared to Kehena, and most of the tree-cover and landscaping you'll see there has been done by the residents. Some folks prefer the sparse vegetation to being in a dense forest, and in the Kehena-to-Seaview area you certainly have your choice.

Although this may be just our opinion, we feel that Palisades is a bit more, well, let's say civilized than Seaview. There are some residents of Seaview who have been there for many years and they resent what some folks think of as progress. They would prefer to keep things as they have always been and they feel that the newcomers are expecting to clean up the community to the detriment of the old-timers. There is a community association of sorts, and we've heard some very colorful stories about the rather bizarre goings-on at their meetings.

Be careful here, and do your homework!

Kurtistown, Mountain View, Glenwood

Kurtistown, Mountain View and Glenwood are all small communities on Highway 11, the Volcano Highway. They are all situated along the Highway starting just *mauka* of Kea'au. Surrounding the residential areas are the small farms that supply most of the produce that you'll find in our farmers' markets and some of what you'll find in the stores. (Curiously, most of the produce in Hawai'i's stores is imported from the Mainland.) The elevation of this area is just high enough that it rains a lot. It's one of those places that on a nice, sunny day, it looks irresistibly green and lush, but careful inspection reveals there are no sprinklers anywhere to keep it that way. If your passion is growing things, especially edibles, you couldn't find a more prolific place. If you aspire to having a small organic farm, look no farther. Home prices are quite reasonable, but since the size and quality of the homes and the land they are on vary so much it's difficult to quote actual numbers. This is one of those places you'll need to feel for yourself. There are places deep in forest, others on rolling hills with spectacular views, and still others in small tracts of homes. Lot sizes vary from tiny to huge acreages.

Volcano Village

Volcano Village is reminiscent of many cozy, wooded areas of the Pacific Northwest. It's usually cool and foggy or rainy, also like those parts of the Pacific Northwest. There are attractive, narrow, curvy roads with lovely homes nestled into the woods, and you'll even catch the aroma of wood-burning stoves as you explore here. The ambiance of Volcano Village is not the first thing that comes to mind when one thinks of Hawai'i, but for many it is the real Paradise. You'll find some popular vacation-rentals and B&Bs in this area, and one of the finest restaurants on the Island is in the village.

Homes are moderate in price, ranging from a low of just under $100,000 to as much as you'd like to pay. Compared to the same size home available in many of the Puna subdivisions, Volcano is expensive. It is considered by most of the folks who live there as a pretty exclusive area. At about 26 miles from Hilo, it isn't a very long drive, and the highway is excellent and rarely congested. This is another place you have to really feel for yourself, because it is so very different from any other place on the Island. You have to like cool and rainy weather year 'round, and even be able to deal with some occasional frost in the winter.

On the opposite side of the highway from the Village is Mauna Loa Estates, a development of lots and homes that is more reminiscent of the Lower Puna developments. The streets are straight and at right angles to each other, the homes are sparsely scattered throughout the tract of lots, and the homes are less expensive than those in the Village. So if you like that cooler climate but would rather not be in the dense forest, this might be what you're looking for. The area is forested, but the forest is younger than in the village, so the trees are all smaller. A lot of the area is more brushy than forested, too.

Vog alert! This the first opportunity we've had to introduce you to vog. Vog is volcanic haze, air-pollution that comes from our active volcano. Some of it comes directly from the volcano's vent, but most is from the reaction of hot lava running into the ocean. Vog is a real problem on the Kona side of the Island, as the normal tradewinds carry it off to the west and then around that side. Except for the few days a year when we experience a "Kona wind," a wind coming from the Kona side, we never get vog on the Windward side. If there is an exception to this, it would be Volcano. For some reason, the topography in the area seems to invite a certain amount of vog over the hills into the Volcano area from time to time, so this needs to be considered. Mostly, the negative effect of vog is how it obscures our famous sunsets (and the view in general), but it also has its health hazards. People with any kinds of respiratory problems should avoid vog exposure.

Wood Valley

Wood Valley is a mystical, magical, peaceful and quiet place. It's a small rural community nestled into a valley that affords some awesome views.

There aren't often many homes or even lots for sale in this area, and when they come on the market they are usually fairly pricey compared to other rural properties. The prices vary widely depending on the size, location and useful area of the parcel. The whole area is hilly so there isn't a lot of level land.

The nearest town to Wood Valley is Pahala, on Highway 11 and about ten minutes *makai*. Driving time to Hilo is about an hour, so this would not be a good place to live for anyone needing to make frequent trips. The long distance to supplies and jobs has kept Wood Valley sparsely populated and the real estate prices low.

Wood Valley can get vog from time to time if the wind is just right. Most of the time, the only vog you'll experience is what you can see of it in the view toward the ocean, but occasionally, it does drift up into the valley.

Although this whole region is fairly dry, Wood Valley does enjoy some afternoon and evening rains.

Wood Valley is home to the Wood Valley Buddhist Temple and Retreat Center, an unbelievably beautiful and tranquil place nestled into a verdant hillside. There is a year 'round schedule of all kinds of spiritual and healing-arts retreats and workshops.

Pahala

Here are some real housing bargains! Pahala, situated about halfway between Volcano and Na'alehu, is a sleepy little town of mostly older homes. It has a quaint charm and is neat and tidy, even though many of the homes show their ages. This is another of the many casualties of the sugar industry, and unlike some towns that have picked themselves up and developed a new source of income and commerce, for this one, time seems to be standing still. The way things are going here, it won't be too long before this turns around, because the bargains are just too good.

Older homes in very restorable condition go for give-away prices, like well under $100,000. Rents here are also cheap, often under $500 a month for a decent 3-bedroom home. Of course, with the hour's drive to Hilo, Pahala is best suited to those who won't need to make the trip often.

It's hot and dry here most of the time, so this is a place for sun lovers!

A 10-minute drive will take you to Punalu'u Black Sand Beach, which is a great place for swimming and playing in the surf. The proximity to the beach, Volcanoes National Park and a golf course make it seem like some day this, too, will become developed as a tourist destination. Want to start a B&B?

Na'alehu and Vicinity

Na'alehu is a picturesque, friendly little village that is about as typically "local style" as you'll find anywhere on the Island. The part of town you'll see while driving though is a just a few blocks of small businesses, a few homes right on the highway, a church and a big park on the *makai* side of the road. There are also homes and farms tucked away in the areas around the village.

Na'alehu is a long way from supplies, entertainment and just about everything else, so you have to really like being out in the country to make your home here. The drive to either Hilo or Kailua is well over an hour, and these are the only sources for major supplies, hardware and other staples of day-to-day living.

The weather is usually dry and warm. You'll almost always find some properties for sale in the Na'alehu area, and the prices reflect the long distance from the Island's two major business districts.

H.O.V.E.

Hawai'ian Ocean View Estates, most often simply called Ocean View or HOVE, is a huge tract of lots, mostly on an old lava flow with spotty vegetation. Barren is a word that comes to mind. Properties here are among the least expensive on the Island, and among the reasons for this are the long drive to Kailua-Kona, the topography, and the air-quality. Often, vog hangs in the air here so that the ocean, only a short distance away, is barely visible through the haze. People with respiratory problems need to be especially aware of the locations of vog areas when trying to assess a future home site. It is possible to be in one of these places on one of the few days when there is very light vog (or even none), and jump into buying a property only to find out later about the vog.

Immediately adjacent to HOVE, on the *mauka* side of the highway, are two smaller subdivisions: Kona Kai View Estates and Hawai'ian Ranchoes. The weather for this whole area is best described as hot and dry.

The whole portion of the Island from HOVE to Kailua gets heavily impacted with vog a lot of the time, but there have been spells of several when the volcano stopped pumping lava into the ocean and the sky was brilliant and clear. As lovely as West Hawai'i is during one of these rare times, this is not a good time to be looking for real estate!

The vog thing seems to bother some people a lot more than it does others. We've talked to tourists and friends who had just experienced the Kona side for the first time and some say they didn't even notice it, while others complain about sore throats and no more "famous Kona sunsets." Many of the people who live there year 'round say, "What vog?" Even so, not being able to see the ocean horizon trough the haze, and then the occasional bad-day vog warnings on the radio make it hard to ignore that vog is a reality for many. You just have to experience it for yourself to see if might be a problem for you.

On Toward Kailua Town

The South Kona area is blossoming with new homes in many tiny subdivisions, most of them being up near the highway. Some are just *mauka* of the highway and others reach from the highway as far downslope as the terrain will accommodate. Several are so steep that traversing the main roads is right on the edge of scary. There are even a few small beaches along this route, but they are mostly at the ends of long, steep, twisty roads. The home prices here are attractive and if you like the environs, this is a good place for bargain hunting.

Honaunau, Captain Cook, Kealakekua and Holualoa

We're now well up on the Kona side of the Island. We'll group these areas together because they are all in the same general area. Honaunau is a residential area between the highway and the ocean and has many inviting, twisty streets with homes ranging from humble to extravagant. Homes here start at around $100,000 and the sky is the limit on the high end of prices. It's mostly hilly with little level land available, but with good tree cover in most places. Many of the homes here, even the humble ones, feature beautiful tropical landscaping.

Captain Cook and Kealakekua are centered on the highway that runs upslope from the ocean through this whole area. Ocean views from up here are "distant" views, but some are spectacular anyway. The cooler temperatures at this elevation make the area desirable for those who don't deal well with the often over 90 degree temps closer to sea-level. This whole stretch of highway is a commercial zone, so residents can find shopping, restaurants and even hardware, furniture and appliances. There are many coffee farms around here, and some are usually on the market at any given time. Most of them are small operations of a few acres with a home.

Again, the caveat here is the vog. When the Kona side gets a dose of vog, this is the area that gets it the worst. On the bad days, it is difficult to see the ocean at all from here. It would be a good idea to spend some time if you become interested in possible residence in this area.

This whole region is the one remaining place where you will still find a lot of leasehold properties for sale. Especially up in "coffee country," which covers most of the properties on both sides of the highway, there are many small acreages with homes and coffee farms. When you see a listing for a three acre producing coffee farm with a nice home, all for an unbelievable price, it's most likely a leasehold property. We cover the caveats of leasehold properties elsewhere, but please check out any leasehold offerings very carefully! Depending on your personal situation, a leasehold property could work well for you but again, many of the leases are near their renegotiation times and the new "adjusted" rates can be real deal-breakers.

Just a little farther up the road and immediately *mauka* of Kailua Village is the small, picturesque community of Holualoa. Known as an artist's community, this area is hilly and again, has little level land. The main street (the highway that runs through all of the preceding communities) has a number of galleries, all featuring the excellent works of local-area artists. There is also a fine coffee shop renown for mouth-watering pastries, fruit smoothies and well-prepared espresso drinks. Homes here are not often on the market and when they do become available they are usually upward of $200,000. Occasionally, though, smaller or fixer-upper places come on the market for about half that amount. This is one of those places where it's good to talk to the local folks if you're serious about finding a home. As you visit the galleries and the coffee shop, ask questions about any properties for sale. You might just be pleasantly surprised!

Kailua-Kona

Kailua-Kona, Kailua Village, Kailua and Kona are all names that you will hear used to describe the same area. The reason for the confusion is that Kona is actually a District (much like a county on the Mainland) and the tourist destination of Kailua Village just happens to be in that district. So for some, it's "We're going to Kona this year for our vacation." The actual name of the Village is Kailua, but since there is also a "Kailua" on several of the other Islands, that's a source of confusion in itself. "Kailua-Kona" is actually an accurate way of describing the town of Kailua, as it shows the name of the town ahead of the name of the District it's in. In the interests of clarity, we have chosen "Kailua Village" to describe the immediate village area that includes all the hotels, restaurants, condos and tourist facilities. Within the Village, we also include all of the residential subdivisions listed below. "Kailua-Kona," includes all of the above plus the subdivisions both industrial areas that are toward the airport from the Village. Whew!

Ali'i Drive, Kailua Town

To live in Kailua-Kona, one must like the faster-moving tourist energy that is pervasive there. We enjoy being there for an occasional day or two, but then when we get all wound up in that energy it feels so good to come back home to the peace and tranquility of the Hilo side. For sure, there are those who love this kind of ambiance, and perhaps Kailua-Kona is their paradise. If you are one of these people, there are usually a few affordable homes available in and around the Village.

If you like the hotter, drier climate near the ocean, there are also homes within a few blocks from the water that fall into the affordable category. They'll be either small or in need of repairs, or both. We've seen some great offerings on multi-family places in this area, too, which could offer a home with a built-in income. Upslope, the vicinities of Captain Cook and Kealakekua offer cooler temperatures and less noise and traffic. It also often rains here in the late afternoons and evenings, further keeping things greener and cooler.

Keep in mind that the prices of nearly everything you'll ever need are higher here than when you get out of tourist-land. To some that could add up to a significant amount after a while, particularly if you need to drive a lot and have to buy gasoline at tourist prices. If you are skilled in frugal living, though, you can still manage it here once you find an affordable home.

The residential subdivisions close in to Kailua Village are where you will find the best home buys. We've included most of them here so that you'll know where they are if you see homes advertised. Some are very upscale, but they'll be easy to identify when you look at the listed home prices. After a while, you'll get to recognize the subdivision names that always have the lowest prices. As in most subdivisions, the lots tend to be small and the homes fairly close together. Because of the hilly terrain immediately *mauka* of the Village, many of even the lowest priced homes have great ocean views. Here's a list of the subdivisions close in to Kailua Village:

Kailua Estates	Kuakini Makai
Kona Heights	Kamani Trees
Kailua Estates	Kilohana Kai
Kona Heights	Kailua View Estates

Kona Vistas	Alii Kai
Kona Orchards	White Sands Estates
Ilolani	Kahalu'u Beachlots
Lono Kona	Kahalu'u Bay Villas
Aloha Kona	

The residential subdivisions on the airport side of the Village are-with a few exceptions-less expensive than the ones we just explored. Most are accessed from the highway going from the Village up to Kamuela (Waimea), Highway 190, also known as Mamalahoa Highway. Most are on steep hillsides, making possible some expansive views but no level land. Note that the views here are "expansive" rather than "great." Of course, that's a personal opinion, but from up in these hills, the view is mostly barren lava flows, the airport and on those days when you can see it through the distant haze, the ocean.

When looking at homes in these areas, pay attention to any difficulty you (or the real estate salesperson) might be having getting in and out of driveways. Some of the roads are actually steep enough to make this a concern. Visualize yourself living there and dealing with the lack of level land around your home. To some this is not an issue, but to others it can be a big deal after a while, especially to those who enjoy puttering around in the garden. The names of these subdivisions are as follows:

Kona Acres	Kona Wonderview
Kona Heavens	Kona Highlands
Pu'uhonua Estates	Keahole Heights

Makaula	Kona Macadamia
Coastview	.......Acres
Palisades	Harbor View
Kaloko Houselots	Queen Liliuokalani
Kaloko Heights	.......Village
Kona Panoi	Hale Palani
Kona Hills Estates	Kailua Heights
Kealakehe Estates	Jacaranda Gardens
	Paniolo Country

Kawaihae

Kawaihae seems to be extraordinarily ripe for development. It consists of an industrial area that contains shipping docks and fuel-storage facilities, a small boat harbor, a tiny shopping complex, several excellent restaurants and a small housing tract just upslope from the highway. There is an area on the Kona side of Kawaihae being developed for another housing tract, and this is no doubt just the beginning. Kawaihae, the location for the infamous movie, "Waterworld," is in the middle of some of the most spectacular ocean anywhere on the Island. The classic picture-postcard Hapuna Beach State Park is only a five-minute drive toward Kona, as are many other perfect beaches.

These areas, plus the ever-sunny weather, are the big attractions here, and it seems that the availability of fresh water is about all that has kept Kawaihae from becoming another busy resort town. For those who would like to live in or near Kawaihae in the near future, the only option is one of the homes (mostly duplexes) in the little community. These are seldom for sale, and when they do come on the market, they run $150,000 and up. Weather here: hot and dry. If daily sunshine and easy access to world-class beaches are important to you, find a way to live here!

As in each of the places we visit on our tour, earning your living is always a consideration. If you will be among those who need to find a job, this is probably not a good place to live. If you're ready to "bring your job with you," this might indeed be your special place. See Chapter 7, "Income Opportunities."

Hawi and Kapa'au

There is no residential development anywhere north of Kawaihae until you get to the northern tip of the Island. (Well, there is one, but it's so expensive we'll just go right on by.) At the northern end, you'll find the lovely communities of Hawi and Kapa'u. They are close enough together that they seem almost as one. Both were sugar-mill communities, and when the mills closed down, these two enterprising spots fast became artist's communities of some repute. There are many galleries here, and one of the best restaurants on the Island, The Bamboo Restaurant, is a "must-do" when you visit here. Also featured inside the restaurant is another fine gallery of arts, crafts and woodworking.

Residential areas here are sparse, and are found mostly close to the two villages, on both sides of the highway, plus a few subdivisions upslope. The affordable homes in and around Hawi and Kapa'au are limited to what the realtors there like to call "cute starter homes." That's realtor-speak for tiny and probably in need of some serious TLC. These homes, which are mostly old plantation homes with two tiny bedrooms and one tiny bath start at around $150,000, so you would have to have a real passion for the area to make it worthwhile. It's another of those places you just have to feel for yourself. One good way to find leads on homes for sale is to ask around. Ask in the galleries and other little shops. Often these folks know of people who are thinking of selling and haven't yet contacted a realtor. It's worth a try.

Hawi Town

Be aware that it rains a lot here and that you need to be wary of high-wind areas, too. Look at the trees around you, and if they're all permanently bent in the same direction, you'll know there's a strong, prevailing wind there even if the day you are there happens to be calm and serene. The windy spots can be very locally specific (and very windy), and the trees do tell the tale.

From Kapa'au, we'll head up to Waimea. The highway that encircles the Island comes to an abrupt halt a few miles past Kapa'au because from that point on down to the Waipio Valley the terrain is totally road-proof.

Waimea (Kamuela)

There's a story about how come Waimea is also called Kamuela. It seems that back in the early Parker Ranch days when Waimea consisted of a post office and the few stores that supported the ranch population, the postmaster was a gentleman named Kamuela. So when there were letters or packages anywhere else on the Island that were headed for Waimea, the carriers were told to "take this up to Kamuela." After enough years of this, Waimea got to be called Kamuela to the point where the name stuck, which actually relieved a certain amount of confusion since most of the Islands have a town called Waimea.

Here we have a unique higher-elevation (read: cold) village that features two distinct climates. They are known as "Dry Side" and "Wet Side." The Wet Side is the Windward (or Hilo) side, and the weather there is mostly cool, moist and often foggy. The Dry Side transition happens about where the highway from Hawi and Kawaihae (Highway 19) intersects Highway 190, the one going from Hilo to Kona-Kailua.

It really is quite amazing to be driving from the Hilo side, up through this lush, green and rainy forest, then into Kamuela Town (we prefer Kamuela to Waimea) and then as you pass through the little community all of a sudden all you see is miles of dusty-dry range grass and prickly-pear cactus!

Both sides of Kamuela have nice, tidy residential areas. There are occasionally homes available in the $100,000 range and up-way up. There are several small subdivisions on the Wet Side that feature all sizes and styles of homes from tiny cabins to big and lavish estates. In these areas is where you'll find the lowest-cost housing.

The weather on the Wet Side can be warm and pleasant during the summer-month days, but is more often than not cool and wet. A fog lives nearly constantly in the surrounding hills and it flows gently down into these small, forested communities. There are a lot of folks who would live nowhere else, and they enjoy the cool climate and their wood stoves.

On the Dry Side, it seldom rains and it is warmer during the days. The evenings do cool off and are usually 10-20 degrees cooler than at sea level. Summers can bring 78-80-degree days and 50-60-degree nights, but we've experienced 40-degree nights at any time of the year when coming home from the Kona side. We always make sure we have enough gas to get us over the mountain so we won't have to get out of the car in Kamuela! Frosts are not uncommon on winter nights, and those who live in Kamuela keep a supply of warm clothes and a pile of firewood ready year 'round. The normal attire in Kamuela is quite similar to what you would see in Oregon or maybe Seattle; an interesting observation for us folks who live at sea level and are used to shorts and rubber slippers.

If you do your shopping in Kamuela, be prepared to pay more for everything. Gasoline is generally the highest price on the Island, usually about 20 cents higher than Hilo and even higher than in touristy Kailua-Kona. Groceries and even the farmer's market offerings are higher as well.

Honoka'a

A 15-minute downhill drive through some exquisite countryside takes you to the neat little town of Honoka'a. Often, a few minutes before arriving in Honoka'a, you will find yourself driving out from under Kamuela's cloud cover and into bright. clear sunshine.

Another would-be casualty of the sugar industry, this little town picked itself up and turned itself into a tourist attraction and an active and desirable location for living in general. The main street is lined with new and old businesses, including several good restaurants, coffee shops, antique stores, galleries and much more. A star attraction is the Honoka'a People's Theater, a beautifully and lovingly restored old theater that now features many musical and cultural events. The annual week-long music festival brings in musicians from around the world and nearly every night is a sell-out. The old-time flavor of the community has been well preserved while cleaning up the store fronts.

The road to Waipio Valley goes through the town, and the residential areas are scattered all the way from the main highway (Highway 19) to Waipio. Homes are rarely available for under $100,000 here, and most are substantially higher. This is one of the places that if it feels right to you, you would do well to spend some time there and drive every street looking for "for sale" signs. The realtors, while they do a good job finding listings, don't get them all. Some sellers prefer not to go through a realtor, and some of these folks and their offerings can actually be found by asking storekeepers, waitresses and others if they happen to know of any homes for sale. You never know until you try! If you find a for-sale-by-owner (FSBO) property and you would prefer to avail yourself of the services of a realtor, you can still do that, too. The catch is that you (not the seller) will be paying the realtor's commission, although that commission can generally be negotiated down substantially from the prevailing six percent.

Laupahoehoe

We skipped right over some residential areas between Honoka'a and here because they are best found by actually exploring every side road that looks interesting. With a few exceptions, most of them are tiny plantation villages with old, small homes very close together. The exceptions are a few small tracts of newer homes and some small acreages. Kolopa, just a few miles toward Hilo from Honoka'a is all *mauka* of the highway and goes way up into the cooler elevations. There are homes and small farms scattered along this road from the highway all the way to the top. Again, take a drive up the road if you lean toward the cooler elevations and see what it feels like to you. For folks who like the cooler climes, there are some beautiful settings all through this peaceful and quiet area, some with incredible far-reaching views, too.

There really isn't much residential area in Laupahoehoe, but we listed it because of its road right down to the ocean. With the exception of a couple of surf spots near Hilo where rivers run to the ocean, this is one of the only ocean access points along the highway from Honoka'a to Hilo. You can find some homes along the road to the ocean, but be forewarned that this is a very steep road with nearly no level land along its way, and because it is an East-facing cliff, the sun sets early in the afternoon there. The residential portion of Laupahoehoe that is not down this road is mostly *mauka* of the highway and goes up into the hills.

Homes, when they come on the market, vary a lot in price because of the vast differences in size, age, quality and lot-size. They are available here from time to time for under $100,000. The weather is best described as rainy. Even at the lower elevations, because of the East-facing cliffs, this area is nearly always damp. The lush foliage along the road to the ocean is good evidence of the wet climate.

From Laupahoehoe, shopping or any other town activity is a long drive in either direction.

Honomu

Only 12 miles from Hilo, this would be a nice place to live for folks who were going to work in town. Honomu likes to think of itself as an "artist's community," mainly because of the several excellent galleries along the short main street. It's a small community with only a few streets, but homes do show up on the market here and they go for as little as $60,000. Expect to pay twice that for a newer home on a large lot, though, because the lower-priced properties are usually ex-plantation homes on tiny lots. Some of these are really quite nice, though, and depending on your needs, they could serve you well.

This village, and the small commercial area, gets its traffic from the folks driving to Akaka Falls Park, only a few miles farther up the road. This is a small park with an easy one-mile walk through some spectacular scenery and to the viewing point of 400-foot-high Akaka falls. The quaint street lined with galleries and small eateries is on the road to the falls, so many of the tourists stop there.

Papa'ikou

From Honomu to Hilo are several more communities. Pepeekeo, Papai'kou, and Wainaku are all in this area and have older homes available at affordable prices. You'll see newer ones there too, but the prices quickly transcend affordability. If an ocean view is not important to you, you can find newer homes that are still within reach. We've seen some great deals on nice places needing extensive repairs, too. If you have the skills and the inclination for this kind of project, tell your realtor to find some "fixers" for you. Some realtors routinely avoid even showing run-down homes to clients unless asked to do so.

Wainaku is very close to Hilo, so close that the lower portion is only a 10-minute walk from downtown.

These are all worth your while to investigate if you feel comfortable with this kind of environment. It's semi-rural, and spotty in that there are some tacky places right in among the nicer homes. Many of these homes have great views of the beautiful Hilo Bay.

If you are attracted to this part of the Island but are looking for something a little more upscale, look for listings especially on the *makai* side of the highway, as this is where most of the nicer homes are. Again, you'll find small homes needing repairs right in there with the big, pricey ones. Some incredible bargains can be found in this area with a little perseverance.

Full Circle

Well, we're back in beautiful Hilo, so let's stop in at Bear's Cafe for an excellent cappuccino and some "talk story." We've gone all the way around this awesome Island now, and we've just touched on a few of the possibilities for affordable living. In between every two places we've visited, there are many more places hiding. Some, you'll never find no matter how long you live here, but the more you search, the more you'll discover.

We suggest that you collect your feelings about all the places you've visited so far, weed out the ones that you didn't care about at all, and slowly narrow your vision to a few locations. At that point, the only way you'll know where to call "home" is to spend some time in each remaining place. Feel the place—listen to your heart. Talk to people. Ask questions. Spend some time there at different hours of the day. See how quiet it is at night; how the ocean sounds from there. Be sure to drive every street nearby, too. Better yet, walk the area to get an even better feel of it.

We once found this incredible home near Wainaku that we were ready to buy. We did our recommended drive all around every little nook and cranny and guess what we came across? A hog farm! The day we were there was windless (unusual) and this stinky hog farm was upwind of the place we were considering. The stench within a quarter mile of the farm was unreal, so we could only imagine how far it would have carried when the wind came back.

Other nuisances to look for are poultry or other kinds of farms, or even some guy who is raising a yard full of game cocks. This is a popular thing to do in any areas zoned for farming, and a lot of rural Hawai'i falls into that category. How would you like to wake up at five every morning to a hundred crowing roosters? And of course, unless you are a dog-lover and enjoy the sound of barking dogs, be ever vigilant for evidence of nuisance dogs. The signs include not only the dogs themselves, but kennels, dog runs, dog houses, and the ubiquitous local-style "tie-dogs." Tie-dogs are dogs kept on short chains at the corners of a person's property. There is usually a small shelter of some sort and the dogs, if they are serving their intended function, bark continuously, day and night. It is our recommendation to forget any property, no matter how desirable, if there are tie-dogs in the neighborhood. There is generally nothing that can be done to stop nuisance dogs in a neighborhood where most of the people don't find the noise to be a nuisance.

It is our feeling that the most important ingredient of your search should be to listen to your heart. After all the logical decision-making is over with and you think you have it all figured out, let your heart—your intuition—make the final decision.

Liliuokalani Gardens, Hilo

Chapter Five

Making the Big Move

You've done the hard part. After a lot of thoughtful research, you've picked out the area of the Island where you want to live; you've decided whether to rent or buy and perhaps you've already chosen the exact house and tied up the real estate transaction. Now it's time to organize a smooth and easy transition to Paradise.

> Tip: On a pre-move visit to Hawai'i, be sure to pick up a Big Island telephone directory. It's an excellent resource for all sorts of useful information that will come in handy in planning your move. The phone book also has some of the best street maps you'll find anywhere, covering most areas on the Island.

In the Reference Guide in the back of this book, you'll find some recommended reading on the generic details of organizing a relocation move. We'll cover the basics here and then go into some detail on those things that make a move to an island in the middle of the ocean different from a move across the continent. If you feel a need for more detailed nuts-and-bolts info on moving in general, please check out our recommended titles.

The Plan

When you get all settled into your new Island home, you'll want to be thinking, "It's amazing how everything regarding this move just seems to have fallen into place. It's like it was meant to be." YES! That's the way it will be, and we're going to help the "falling into place" process with some planning tips.

The planning process should start at least a few months before your anticipated move. Matter of fact, the first thing on your list should be to decide the best time of year for the move. If you have school-age children, their timely arrival into the school environment—like between semesters—will be a consideration here. Weatherwise, it doesn't much matter on the Hawai'i end of your move, but the weather at your present home might be a big factor. Here, the weather is almost always moving-friendly, but the winter months do bring in storms and more rain. This will usually not present a problem for you, because your belongings will always be under cover except for the actual process of moving them from the shipping container into your new home. On the other hand, planning a move in winter from where the weather brings ice and snow might be asking for delays. Delays on one leg of shipping your goods can mean a missed connection at the following one.

The next thing you might want to do is decide how you will be shipping your possessions. Most people move their belongings to the Islands by way of shipping-container freight. A little later we'll discuss why some are sorry they did.

If you will be shipping a container-load of household goods, you'll need to get the container to your home for packing, and then from your home to one of the three shipping points to Hawai'i: Seattle, San Francisco or Los Angeles. From there the container goes on a big container-ship to Oahu, on a barge to Hawai'i Island, and then again on a truck to your new home.

We recommend Matson Navigation as your across-the-ocean shipper because we've had dependable and reasonable service from them. You will want to call them (or the shipper of your choice) for rates on full and partial containers, as this is a good starting point for determining how much you'll want to bring with you. Since the container will have to be delivered by truck to your present home for loading (by you or by hired help) and then moved to the freight docks, you'll want to get prices from several trucking firms. Check your yellow pages for options, and then call several and get an idea of their charges. Be certain you're comparing apples and apples, though, and make sure every rate you get is for the same services. For example, some freight rates are by the pound, while others are by the cubic foot.

Once you get these basic rates, you'll be in a better position to decide how much stuff you really want to take with you. Another real consideration in figuring your moving logistics is how far you live from the West Coast. If you are in the Midwest or farther east, it could cost you more to ship your furnishings to the West Coast dock than it will cost from there to Hawai'i. This is when it becomes necessary to do some careful planning on what--and what not to bring with you.

If you decide to bring enough of your household and personal goods that you'll be able to fill up a container, it usually works like this: a trucking firm will bring the container to your home and you will be allowed a few days to pack it. (See "Packing and Unpacking Your Container" below.) Then it will be trucked to the nearest West Coast shipping dock, and from there it will travel by container-ship to Honolulu and from there by barge to Hilo. Another trucking firm will pick up the container in Hilo and take it to your new home, and again you'll be allowed a few days to unload it. When you have it all emptied out, the trucking firm will whisk it away and you will be officially moved in. Simple, huh?

It really is a lot less intimidating than it sounds. You will shop around for the best rate to haul your loaded container from your home to the shipping (across the ocean) docks, and then again from the dock in Hilo to your new home. We have a recommendation in the Resource guide for a good, dependable and reasonable trucking company on this end. They give you ten days to unload, too.

When getting prices from the trucking companies at both ends, ask how long they will leave the container for you. These times vary, and you'll want to try for as much time as possible. A week to ten days seems to be about the normal range of time, and a week should be the minimum you'll accept.

Packing and Unpacking Your Container

Long before the container arrives at your present home, decide on the best place for the trucker to park it. The first consideration is that the spot needs to be level or you'll have nightmares trying to stack and load boxes and especially heavy items. In some cases, it is possible to back the container close enough to the building to be able to use ramps from your porch directly into the container, making loading as easy as possible. Depending on your particular circumstances, it might even be feasible to remove a railing or other obstacle to facilitate ramps directly from the container into the house. Failing this luxury, make sure the trucking company supplies you with a long, sturdy ramp so you can easily wheel your heavy items into the container. Of course, all of these considerations apply at both your existing home and your new Island home.

Do not be tempted to use car-type jacks to level the container! Far better to check the location for level before the driver gets there and if necessary, level a spot in advance. Any dirt or gravel fill will have to be thoroughly compacted, though. Remember, that container can weigh up to five tons when loaded.

Another option if only a few inches of leveling is required is to have some sturdy planks available for the driver to back onto.

If you don't already own a hand-truck, you will want to ask the trucking company if they can supply one for you. If not, you'll have to rent or buy one yourself. Good hand trucks are actually inexpensive enough that you might consider just buying one, because after renting one at both ends you'll have pretty much bought one anyway, only you won't own it!

> A tip: if you buy a hand-truck, don't go for the very cheapest because they are often flimsy and flexible enough to be dangerous. You don't need the most expensive one either, so go for the middle-of-the-road variety. "Home Depot" type stores (or even Ace Hardware stores) usually have good ones for around $40.

There are a few important "rules" to packing your container, whether you do it yourself or have somebody do it for you. One is to try your best to get as much stuff all packed and ready to go into the container as possible, but don't load any of it until you have it all ready to go. The reasons for this are that it's so much easier to pack efficiently if you have many different sizes of boxes and other stuff in plain sight to chose from, and also this allows you to make sure the first things in are the things you're the least likely to need right away when you get there.

Some people do better with lists. We are among them and can hardly function without them. If this includes you, start making your packing lists early and separate them into the items you'll need shortly after your arrival and the other things that you won't be needing right away. It's really inefficient and frustrating to have to scrounge through dozens of boxes and move tons of material several times to find the things you need. Those, by the way, will always be in the boxes at the bottom of the pile.

Another thing that helps a lot is to mark each box with its contents, or at least where the contents came from. For example, "dining room," "office," and like that. It's also helpful to mark each box on at least two sides so that the label will always be visible even when the box is still deeply embedded at the bottom of a huge stack of other boxes. You will end up moving some of your belongings several times before it's all done, but why do it more often than necessary? Let's plan to keep the work and frustration to a minimum.

In packing the container, it's important to pack it as tightly as possible. Keep all of your bedding available for padding between pieces of furniture. We kept all of our books available to fill small spaces, too. We would take a stack of books the right size and wrap them in a brown paper bag, and then use that package as a filler to keep things from shifting in the container. The less movement your packing allows, the less damage you'll get in your possessions. Remember, that container is going to be bounced down highways, picked up with cranes at the docks, loaded and unloaded into ships and barges, and floated across the ocean through whatever storms and rough seas nature has in store at the moment. Pack every nook and cranny, and even fill drawers and every other available space. You'll be glad you did when you get the container nearly full and there's still this big pile left to go into it.

Pack the heaviest items near the front (the doors are on the back) or in the middle of the container-not at the back. Of course, load the least-easily-damaged and the most crush-resistant items at the bottom and the most fragile at the top. Remember, you'll be stacking nearly eight feet high, and that puts a lot of weight on the things at the bottom of the load. The most important thing to keep in mind is to pack so that there can be no movement inside. Get a visual of this gnarly giant picking up your container and shaking it vigorously. Now pack so that nothing will bounce around inside when he does that, and you'll be fine. You'll know you did well when you unpack and there is nothing at all broken or damaged. A friend who recently moved over packed most of her belongings in commercially-available moving boxes of all the same size making loading the container much easier!

> Tip: the last things to go into the container should be the hand truck and any tools you might need to remove doors or other obstacles that can make unloading easier at your new home. Minimum tools would be a claw-hammer, hefty regular screw driver for removing hinge pins, a Phillips screwdriver and if there are any railings or the like that will need to come off, a small crow-bar.

Unpacking the container when it arrives is the fun part! After getting it as conveniently located as possible, carefully open the container doors, watching for anything that might have shifted in transit and is leaning against the door. This is when you will appreciate all the time you spent marking your boxes before you loaded them! Now you can have all those eager helpers take each box into the room where it will need to end up. If you have a big empty space somewhere, like a lanai, it's a good idea to stack the boxes you won't need right away in such a way that the labels are all readable. Try to stack the boxes against a wall but keep the stack only one row deep. That way you'll always be able to see everything without having to move anything else first.

Be sure to leave yourself an ample path for any large items like furniture or appliances. Remember it takes a lot of room to navigate big pieces on a hand truck. Then when you get the last box out of the container, take a break and go jump in the ocean for a while!

What and What NOT to Bring With You

OK, now that you've got the container details down, let's talk about saving a whole lot of money and hassle by not even needing a container at all! There are a lot of things that are easy to replace here in Hawai'i and not cost-effective to ship.

Appliances and Other Big, Heavy Stuff

Appliances are big, heavy, hard to move and easily damaged in shipping, and cost about the same here as they do in most mainland areas. Unless your appliances are very dear to you and maybe you just bought them, you'd do better to leave them behind. You could either sell them at your mega-garage-sale, or include them in the sale of your house, if indeed you're selling your house. It is important to figure in the cost (and inconvenience) of all the shipping, packing and handling when figuring the cost-effectiveness of selling vs. shipping. In other words, don't just figure how much you feel your present appliances are worth compared to how much it will cost for new ones when you get here. To come up with a real figure you need to subtract all of the moving-related costs from their present value.

Example: You're considering your washer, dryer and fridge. They're all about two years old and you paid $1400 for three appliances, so let's say they're worth $1000 now. Shipping them will add about $400 to your moving expenses, and new ones will cost you another $1400 in Hawai'i.

If you ship them over, your total investment in the three appliances will now be $1800 ($1400 purchase price plus $400 shipping). If you sell them for $1000 and replace them here for another $1400, your total investment will also be $1800 ($400 depreciation on the old ones plus $1400 purchase of new appliances). The bottom line is that the cost is the same, but if you sell them you've saved yourself a lot of hassle, plus you end up with brand new appliances again. And the new ones will most likely be delivered to your home for free by the store where you buy them. Obviously, this is just an example and the figures might not be representative, based mostly on the condition of your present appliances, but you get the idea. Another point in all this is that moving your appliances might just be the deciding factor in whether or not you even need to use a container. If it is, it becomes a lot more attractive to leave them behind.

Furniture and Other Household Goods

Furniture is not so easy a decision. For a lot of folks, a change to Island life inspires a change in home decor as well. For example, if you've been living with a houseful of heavy antique furnishings and this feels like the time to switch to a new, light, bright tropical ambiance, this is definitely the time to sell the antiques. Another consideration on antiques (or a lot of other wooden furniture) is that they often don't do well in tropical humidity. We've seen nice vintage furnishings come apart at the seams with the change in climate. Newer furnishings that use composition-board in their construction are also not very well suited for this climate.

With these things in mind, you'll have to decide if your furniture is special enough to you (like for sentimental reasons) to bring it along anyway. New furnishings tend to be expensive here, and there aren't a lot of choices in the way of stores. Hawai'i's itinerant population does, however, make for lots of garage sales when people move back to the Mainland. Chapter 6 reveals the secrets of finding the best deals in new and pre-owned furniture.

As for the rest of your belongings, again, it's decision time and from here on in it'll be on an item-by-item basis. One extreme is to sell your home (if you are a home owner) furnished, or even partly furnished. You could sell it all, right down to the spoons in the kitchen, and start over when you arrive here. It all depends on what you have, how dear it is to you and what it would cost to replace it. We've known quite a few people who decided that since this is such a complete lifestyle change anyway, they would leave it all behind and start fresh here. Of course, if you are attached to the things you've been living with for years and would like to keep them in your life, by all means ship them over.

We'll just toss this in for consideration: We have some vacation rentals. We figure that it costs us right around $1000 to completely furnish a two-bedroom home with moving-sale furnishings, new bedding and bath supplies, and new kitchen appliances and utensils.

Here's some food for thought: Among all the people we've talked to about this, there isn't one (including ourselves) who didn't say they brought over way too much and if they had it to do over they would have sold most of everything before moving. It really does simplify the move and cuts the costs to nearly nothing. If you pared your bring-along stuff to the minimum, you could actually bring some of it as check-in luggage and ship the rest in Priority Mail cartons. Each passenger is allowed two seventy-pound boxes, so for a couple, that's 280 pounds of stuff. Priority mail is expensive, to a point, but maybe not when you figure the charges are from your door there to your door here, and your belongings will arrive in a few days. Remember, shipping by the conventional means, your goods travel by truck to the West Coast docks, by container ship to Honolulu, by container barge to Hawai'i Island, and then again by truck to your door. The time enroute is from four to six weeks from your old home to your new one. Also, you are responsible for the arrangements with each of the shippers; it doesn't just happen automatically. We've talked to people here who did indeed ship a big pile (like a full pickup truck load) of boxes by Priority Mail and ended up paying a few hundred dollars instead of a few thousand--and all the attendant inconvenience-- of shipping a houseful by container.

Clothing

Clothing might not seem like a big issue, but when you consider the amount of clothes the average person owns, it can become a big issue. Shipping all that stuff over here isn't the only thing, either; you'll find that because most folks here don't own or need a lot of clothes, closets are, by Mainland standards, diminutive. We pared down our clothing to what we thought was the basic minimum of necessities, and we still ended up taking most of what we brought to the local thrift shops. For even a couple, this can amount to some big boxes to ship, and if the goal is to make this move as economical as possible, then we need to ship as little as possible.

OK, what will we really need to bring? It depends on several factors, mostly on what climate you've chosen for your home here, and then your basic tastes in apparel.

The first issue is easy. Unless you'll be living in the mountains, like Kamuela or Volcano, you won't need anything as toasty as a sweatshirt except for those rare occasions when you decide to go up to those frigid climes.

So what will you need here in the way of clothes? Just picture yourself living where the temperature rarely drops below 70 degrees. The days range from the low 70s to the high 80s, and the nights can drop into the 60s during the coldest months. The humidity is fairly high all year 'round, so cool, light clothes are in. Normal attire for most folks on most days here is shorts, a cool top or shirt and the traditional "rubber slippers." On the Mainland those slippers are also known as thongs or flip-flops. Most people wear the $2.95 disposable variety here, and for more formal occasions, one can step up to the $10 kind.

One good reason to adopt rubber slippers for your everyday footwear is the local custom of never, ever wearing shoes into a house. It is considered rude to wear shoes inside a home here, and it's a nice custom that's easily adopted, especially if you can simply kick off your slippers before entering somebody's home.

We still get a warm-fuzzy feeling coming to a friend's home for a party or other social engagement and seeing dozens of pairs of slippers in front of the door. The trick is to leave with the same ones you arrived in!

What about those "special occasions?" Even at the theater, a nice restaurant or at parties, people dress very casually here. By mainland standards, very, VERY casually.

You'll more than likely never have occasion to wear any of those dozens of pairs of fancy shoes again, and most of the clothes you used to consider as "casual" before would make sure everyone knows you're a *malihini* (newcomer) wherever you go. Perhaps the best way to decide what to bring in the way of clothes is to carefully observe what the folks who live here wear when you come on your next visit. You might be surprised!

> Tip: Unless you are very attached to your leather goods, best not bring them to Hawai'i. This holds true anywhere in the Islands, too. Leather simply does not get along with the humidity here.

A scenario: You hang your expensive leather jacket in the closet and then a few months later you're going to a concert up in Volcano. Terrific! A chance to wear that old favorite jacket. Surprise! You get it out of the closet and it's all covered with a greenish-white furry mold. Yuk! After duly expressing your reaction to this sight, you get out some rags and brushes and spend half an hour cleaning every fold and crevice, only to watch it get even worse the next time it has to spend some time in the closet.

There is a cure, if you must keep leather goods. You can buy electric closet-heaters here to keep the humidity in your closets under control. They consume only about ten to twenty watts of power, but even so, if left on full time that can add a few dollars a month to your electric bill. The other option is to keep your leather in a very well-ventilated place that gets daily sunshine. Mildew and mold do not like sunshine in any quantity.

We've actually seen fine leather disintegrate if left in a tight closet long enough, so please consider giving all that leather to your best friend as a farewell gesture.

Your Car(s)

Should you ship your car? Only if it's very special, very dear to you, and if adding the shipping costs to what you have invested in the car still leaves you in a favorable position financially. Cars and trucks are not really any more expensive here than there. If you would like to see some real-time prices, on the Internet visit autotrader.com, enter the make and model of your (or any other) car, enter your zip code and search for ads. Then do the same thing only with a Hawai'i zip code. (Hilo is 96720.) Depending on where you live, the results might surprise you. Another way to find a representative cross-section of car prices here is to check the on-line classifieds in the Big Island's two newspapers. They're both listed in the Resource Guide.

Currently the rate Matson charges for shipping a car is just under $900. Bear in mind, though, that this is the rate from the West Coast dock, so you'll also need to figure how you'll get the car to that point. There are vehicle-moving companies that will transport your car, and also "auto drive-away" companies who hire qualified drivers (?) to drive your car cross-country. You could also drive it yourself, of course, on your way to the airport. You just need to schedule your departure from either San Francisco, Seattle or Los Angeles and get a ride from the dock to the airport. Depending on where on the Mainland you live and the size of your family, this could save you a worthwhile chunk of your airfare to Hawai'i. You'll need to rent a car for a while, though, as the shipping takes four to six weeks. Car rentals are reasonable, though, and monthly rates are available. Another way to go, and one used my quite a few people, is to buy yourself an inexpensive car as soon as you arrive, and sell it when yours gets here.

About the only real advantage we can see in shipping over a car rather than buying one when you get here is that if you live in a very dry area where cars do not rust, you will be ahead of the game in that area. Cars do rust here, depending on your location and how you take care of them. Any day of the week, you'll see cars here that are so full of rust holes you have to wonder what's holding them together. Some of these cars might be only a few years old, too. Then on the other hand, there are lots of antique car enthusiasts here who have very old cars in like-new condition. They take car of their cars. We take reasonable care of our cars and one of ours at present is 13 years old and has no visible rust. The trick is we don't leave them parked right by the ocean, and when we do expose them to a lot of salt spray, we wash them with plenty of soap when we get home. Keeping your car well waxed helps, too.

Anyway, if your car is "just a car," and not something near and dear to you, we would recommend selling it and replacing it when you arrive here. Of course, all this presumes you're not going to "sell" your car to your dear brother-in-law for half of what it's worth and then pay full price for a replacement when you get here! If you get top dollar for your car there, you'll be able to replace it here for about the same price, again saving the nearly $900, the bother of shipping it and the four-to-six week wait.

This is definitely going to be an adventure, and some careful pre-move planning can make it an enjoyable one.

Traveling Light

If you decide you'd like to sell nearly everything and travel light, you have several options. One, of course, is the All American Garage Sale. Everybody loves a garage sale, and you can sell a lot of stuff at a sale in the right areas. The right areas are those where it's easy for people to find you. The down-side of garage sales is that almost always, all the good stuff is gone in a flash and then you sit there for the rest of the day staring at boxes and boxes of trinkets, dishes, clothes and toys, all of which you will still own at the end of the sale. Bummer.

Here's a better idea: In your nearest-city phone book, look up "auctions." There are auctions all over the country that specialize in liquidating household goods. We've used these companies with a great deal of success on three occasions now. Believe it or not, the average price they got for our stuff at auction was at least double what we would have ever asked for it at a garage sale. They take their 30% off the top and you still win. Where you really win is that they sell everything, down to the last tiny item. They cleverly group all your little insignificant things into batches of items and the bidders have to bid on the group. They always put some neat teaser in the top of the box, so if you want that item you have to buy the whole box. People go nuts at these auctions. It really is amazing. We've gone to watch a couple of them for entertainment after the last time they sold our stuff for us at unbelievable prices.

If you have some nice antiques, contact several antique dealers and find one who likes the kind of things you have and will take them on consignment. When we left the Mainland, we took a whole houseful of nice European antique furniture to a dealer and left it on consignment. For the next two years, we just kept getting these terrific checks in the mail for pieces they had sold-again for twice and sometimes three times what we thought the pieces were worth.

OK, if you've pared down the shipping needs to what you can take with you and ship by Priority Mail, you're that far ahead. If you've decided no, you would rather keep most of your houseful of furnishings, then we would like to remind you to consider carefully whether they will be appropriate to your new lifestyle. So often, we hear folks talk of the money they could have saved by not shipping over all the furnishings that they ended up replacing when they got here. Again, shipping or selling your present furniture and appliances can be the decision-maker in whether or not you need to bear expense of using a container.

Last But Not Least: Taking Your Pets

This is a sticky subject and one that's not fun to even bring up. Taking pets to Hawai'i's is expensive and is at the very least, a hassle. Especially for the pets. Nobody seems to know if there is any real validity to Hawai'i's stated reasons for the Big Deal, and many seem to feel it's a create-a-job thing along with a nice revenue producer for the State. But enough of that; let's stick with the facts.

What we know is that there is a quarantine period for all pets, and that period depends on what preparations you made long in advance of moving. The newly revised rules have reduced the quarantine period for dogs and cats to 30 days, although it is still 120 days for those under a year old.

Briefly, you must have a $17 microchip implanted in the animal before it arrives in Hawai'i. (This sounds really awful, but we've yet to hear a complaint from any pet owners we've talked to.) Then your vet needs to draw a blood sample and have it analyzed by a lab at Kansas State University to see if it has an adequate antibody level. Kansas State will then send the test results to the Quarantine Station. The reason for the microchip is so that Quarantine personnel can compare the microchip numbers with those of the test results. You need to allow up to 120 days for the implantation and test data to be processed, so it's best to get an early start on this. Delaying can mean having to leave your pet for the longer quarantine period.

If you need info on quarantine, please check the Resource Guide for complete access info for the Hawai'i Quarantine Station. They will send you the latest info packet, and it is important to get up-to-date information as the rules change from time to time-as do the fees. As of this writing, the fees for both dogs and cats is a whopping $555. For the 120 day quarantine, the fees are $1080. Also as of this writing, there is talk of dismantling the entire quarantine program. It seems that in the entire history of the program there has not been one single case of rabies and besides, there seems to be no medical or scientific justification for the quarantine or the insane fees.

Yes, it all seems very strange to hold up the folks who would bring loving and cared-for pets with them, when enforcement for strays and spaying is largely ignored here. It's a big decision, and a lot of it has to do with the age of your pets and how well they will be able to tolerate the time in quarantine. If there is an unpleasant issue in moving to the Islands, this is it.

Scenes typical of many East Hawaii subdivisions

Chapter Six

Shopping: Keeping the Costs Down

"**G**roceries are so expensive in Hawai'i! How could I ever afford to feed my family?" We hear it over and over, and even from folks who have lived here for a while. They back up their claims by quoting Safeway's prices for milk, cereal and other packaged goods. Well, yes they're right. If you need to feed your family with imported, packaged, processed groceries, you will have a big food bill. But wait a minute . . . we're in Hawai'i! There are lots of farms here and we can buy fresh tomatoes and other delicious and nutritious produce year 'round!

We can buy a dizzying array of veggies and fruits at the local farmer's markets for half of what they cost at Safeway, and many of them are organic and they're all fresh. Fresh fish is available from some of the farmer's markets, from small local shops, from the grocery stores and even from the fishermen themselves right out of their coolers on their trucks alongside the road!

We do most of our shopping at the Pahoa and Hilo Farmer's Markets. We buy fresh fish at the Hilo Farmer's Market or at one of the grocery stores if the price is right. Fish prices can vary from day to day depending on the catch, so we buy what there is the most of, which is usually the least expensive. We don't buy milk at Safeway for nearly $6 a gallon when we can buy it at any number of other stores for $3.79. We don't buy fish for $8 per pound when the catch is low, but when there's lots of it and the price is down to $3.50, we stock up. Our total grocery bill is substantially less than it ever was when we were on the Mainland, and the food we get is a whole lot better. Ever taste one of those pinkish-gray orbs they sell as "tomatoes" in the markets? At the Farmer's Market, the beautiful deep-red tomatoes were picked ripe that morning or the day before and are scrumptious!

There are other, more creative ways to obtain in-season fruits and veggies, too. Like instead of paying nearly $3 a pound for mangoes at the supermarket, we drive down to the Red Road and pick up as many as we can use off the ground. After you live here for a while, you'll likely never again pay for things like avocados, mangoes, pomelos (Hawai'ian-style grapefruit), lilikoi (passion fruit), guavas, or any of the other goodies that grow in abundance here. After a while here, you'll discover all the "secret" places where you can pick up all the fruit you want off the ground or even off of trees the owners don't care to harvest themselves. And even if you must buy at the Farmer's markets, how about papayas at seven for a dollar? Or avocados at four for a dollar with several varieties to choose from. No, our groceries are not expensive.

We never have figured out the reason for the astronomical prices of boxed cereals here, except that as long as people keep buying them at those prices, I suppose the message to the suppliers is to keep supplying them at those (and higher) prices. If you insist on buying packaged, processed (not good for you anyway) foods, then get them at Costco in the huge sizes for about the same price as the little boxes at the supermarket.

We have Costco, Wal*Mart, K-mart and other Mainland-style outlets here for those who like that kind of shopping. Costco is a genuine savings on a lot of things, and ours has a building-materials department, too. If yours is a big family and you have the freezer space, you will do well there. In Hilo, there is also a "Cost-U-Less" store, which we think of as "Costco Lite." They have a lot of the same things to offer at slightly higher prices. The store is a warehouse-type operation like Costco, but a fraction of the size and an inventory accordingly smaller. Still, they do offer substantial savings over normal market prices for many bulk-packaged items.

The Big Rule of Hawai'i Shopping

The one Big Rule here is to shop around. We find that there can be huge price differences from one store to another for the same item. It doesn't matter what it is, either. Auto parts, hardware, appliances or groceries all qualify. We find it isn't uncommon to get price differences of 50% or more from one supplier to another. It really does pay to make a few phone calls before buying anything costing more than a few dollars. Another tip: There is no consistency to the price differences, either. One store may have your favorite laundry detergent on sale this month, and another will next month. Shop around, and watch the sale flyers in the newspapers.

Another Big Rule: if you find an item you need on a regular basis and the price is right, buy a bunch of them! For various reasons that include shipping, storage and other factors, stores here do not manage their inventories like they do on the mainland. You can go into Longs Drugs and find your favorite shampoo, for example, at half of what you've been paying for it elsewhere. So you buy one and decide to remember next time you need shampoo, get it at Longs. Bad move. Next time you need shampoo, Longs might just not carry that brand any more. Same thing at Costco. You go there and they have this terrific deal on HP printers. You tell yourself, well, I'm coming back here next week anyway, I'll pick up one then. And then next week they're all gone and the manager tells you sorry, no more.

It seems like a lot of attractively-priced merchandise here is a one-shot deal. So when you find something you need on a regular basis and it isn't perishable, stock up! Even if it's an exception and will continue to be available, it will cost more next month than it does today.

Tip: If you find an item you really need at a great price, even if you were not planning on making the expenditure right now, go for it because it most likely won't be there when you need it.

Take Yourself on a Tour

When you have some free time, take a tour of your nearest (and even the not-so-near) shopping resources. Especially if you will be doing any decorating or remodeling, go visit all of the businesses that provide the things you might need: Hardware stores, building-materials stores, decorating shops, and even the department stores. Price structures are not the same here as on the Mainland, and you might be surprised at what you find. It's a good idea to have some general knowledge of what's available and who carries it if you are to become a frugal shopper here.

Tour the various grocery outlets, too, and get a general idea of overall pricing, inventories, freshness of goods, and just the feeling you get from the different places. Forget everything you've ever learned about shopping on the Mainland; the rules are all different here.

Be sure to find out where the farmer's markets are in your area and visit all of them eventually. Prices vary, especially in the more touristy areas. A general rule is that any markets easily available to tourists will have higher prices than those tucked away and harder to find.

Mail Order vs. Local Shopping

We rely on mail-order for a lot of the things we need, including tools, household goods and any number of specialty items. The Internet has made mail-order so much easier now, what with not even having to have a catalog. You just go to your computer, type in whatever it is you need, and there it is, being offered by numerous vendors.

There is one condition to our shopping mail-order, though, and we like to encourage everyone to follow suit. Please give our local merchants and suppliers first chance at filling your needs. Often, it's just so easy to go to the computer and punch in a few keystrokes. A few days later, your treasure is in the mailbox. But we have lots of stores here who's owners and managers try their best to keep prices as low as possible, not to mention support their families. We always give them first chance and even if the cost is slightly higher, we'll buy local. One thing the slightly higher price will buy you is continued and friendly service should something go wrong. Dealing with defective merchandise bought on-line can be a real headache.

Shipping Costs

Be sure to include shipping costs when comparing prices between mail-order and local purchases, too. Remember that the shipping costs on heavy items can easily use up any savings in the cost of the item itself.

Speaking of shipping, when we order anything that weighs only a two pounds or so, we've learned to ask up-front if shipping by Priority Mail is an option. If the vendor says no, we try somebody else. Consistently, items shipped to us by UPS or FedEx take longer to get here and cost far more. For example, UPS has a minimum charge of around $15 (depending on where the shipment originated on the Mainland), so if you're buying an item that costs $50 or less, that can add significantly to the overall cost. If the item is less than two pounds in weight, Priority Mail will get it here for $3.95 in a few days. FedEx or UPS will cost you their minimum of at least $15 and it could longer to get to you. One caution, though: with the new USPS postal rate hike in effect, the rate difference gets less and less as the parcel-weight increases.

And to be fair, we have received both FedEx and UPS shipments from the Mainland in two days, too, but this is clearly the exception.

Before 9/11, Priority Mail delivery time from the West Coast was usually two days and rarely more than three. Since then, the mail can no longer go on airliners as baggage, so it has slowed a bit. Now, we expect Priority Mail packages in three to five days. Hopefully, that situation will be rectified in the not-too-distant future.

We just received a package of books from Seattle that was shipped FedEx "overnight" and it took a week to get here. One of the reasons is that the FedEx drivers don't seem to know the rural areas and if they have difficulty finding an address they take the package back and send you a notice though the mail! So much for overnight. Actually there is no such thing as "overnight" to the Big Island (or any other outer Island). So-called overnight packages might make it to Oahu overnight, but from there they get shipped to the outer Islands the following day

More on Shopping Local

Our dedication to shopping local extends to avoiding the big discount chains if we can do as well locally. Many of the Mainland biggies are represented here and more are showing up all the time. Hilo just got its Wal*Mart a few years ago; Kailua- Kona has one of those plus a K-Mart nearby. We have found, over and over, that these giants have some of their advertised goods priced well below the local competition, but the bulk of their offerings are often the same or even higher than local prices. Office Max in Hilo is a good example. We have two locally-owned office supply stores in Hilo and both consistently beat Office Max in a lot of their prices. Again, it comes down to shopping around. Shopping around does take some time and effort, but if getting the most out of your hard-earned dollars is important to you, you'll find your time is well spent.

It has been our consistent experience that most items can be purchased here for about the same as mainland prices, at the possible expense or inconvenience of not having what you want at the moment you want it. The trick is to buy when you see it at the right price instead of buying on impulse of what you feel you need at the moment. Planning ahead is a valuable tool in this process. Like if you know you're going to be redecorating your home in the near future, don't wait until the day you start the project to begin looking for what you need. Keep the project in mind as you peruse the sales or browse the stores, and pick up whatever you find at a good price when you find it. Same goes for major purchases like appliances. If you know your washer and dryer are not long for the world, don't wait until one or the other dies and then expect to find a great deal on a replacement. As soon as you decide a replacement is due soon, start looking for the deals. We have the occasional lapse ourselves: We just bought a fridge for a rental a few weeks ago for $750 and this morning's paper listed the same exact item for $549! Ouch! In this case, it was a minor emergency. We had a few weeks notice on this one and shopped all the local sources for the best price. $750 was the best deal going at the time, so we grabbed it. So much for listening to our own advice . . .

For sure, don't make the mistake of taking a note of where you saw an item and then expect to find it there at the same price (or at all, for that matter) when you get around to needing it!

More on Shipping

You'll find some local merchants will automatically charge you a shipping charge on any items they need to order in for you. For example, you go to the appliance store and you look over the large selection of refrigerators. What you really want, though, is one with all the features of the almond-colored one, but in white. The salesman says, no problem, he can have one like that in the store for you in a week. But, he says, there will be a $50 shipping charge to get it here from Oahu. Forget that! There are lots of appliance stores on this Island, and they all love to sell their refrigerators. You will most likely find exactly what you want if you—anyone?—Yes! Shop around!

Then when you do find the exact one you want, try to contain your enthusiasm and be looking at a different one when the salesman approaches you. After he gives you the price on that one, shake your head in dismay and ask him how much for the ugly one--the one you really want. Rarely are prices here set in stone, even at such stores as Sears and Penneys. You can almost always get the store to drop the price, even if only a little, with some creative applied sales resistance. At the very least, get the store to deliver it for free!

The added shipping charge is often valid, but you can avoid it in most instances by finding what you want from somebody else. There's an art to confining your needs to what is available locally. Some folks pick up on this right off, and others fight it forever. Observing local traditions, tastes and styles and adapting them to your own lifestyle can save you a lot of money and frustration. The folks who have the most trouble are those who bring their mainland notions of how things should be done. Like the guy who decides to build a big Spanish-style stucco house in a community of conservative local-style beach homes and then wonders how come he has trouble finding supplies, or help that knows anything about that style of construction.

Home Furnishings and Appliances

New furniture is expensive here, but then it is on the Mainland, too. At this writing, we have no true "discount" furniture stores here, and this would be an excellent business opportunity for anyone so inclined!

What we do have, however, is an itinerant population, so there are lots of moving and garage sales! You have to be prepared to get to there early for the best stuff, but we've seen some terrific deals at these sales. There are a few outlets that deal in surplus hotel furniture, and these are the suppliers of choice for those who have to furnish vacation-rentals here. We've furnished three vacation-rentals very nicely from a combination of garage sales and used hotel furnishings.

Used hotel furnishings are not junk, either. Well, some are, but there are some five-star hotels here and when they replace furnishings, they usually replace all of it and upgrade the entire hotel, meaning that there will be some nearly-unused items in each lot sold. We've bought king-size beds at one of these places, for example, that look and feel like new, and they go for around $125 complete.

Costco also carries a small inventory of furniture, all at great prices. Again, watching the sale flyers in the papers will find you some bargains. The furniture stores do all run occasional sales, and that's the time to buy new.

One more source for new furniture at a discount is the occasional warehouse sale. Some of the dealers will occasionally bring in a huge container load of furniture, usually from Indonesia, and then rent a warehouse to run a "sale" until the supply is gone. Again, watch the papers for these.

For some reason, appliances don't seem to be higher here than on the Mainland. Out of a recent Sunday-Paper Sears ad: A new 18-cubic-foot fridge for $516, a premium washer and dryer for under $700 for the pair, a dishwasher for $260, and any number of new ranges starting at under $400. These prices are representative of any number of appliances stores. There are also several places that sell refurbished appliances for really cheap prices. And again, you can find appliances at garage sales, too.

One caveat on appliances: depending on your location on the Island, many appliances will rust out before they wear out, so buying used means you need to scrutinize for rust. Look at the backs of washers, dryers and ranges, and the tops of the cabinet and doors of refrigerators. That's where the rust usually shows up first.

The same goes for furniture, too. Especially if you will be living anywhere near the ocean, don't even think about buying outdoor furniture made of steel! Pay the few extra dollars and make sure it's all aluminum. Take a small magnet with you when you shop and if it sticks to anything on the furniture (even if it's advertised as being made of aluminum), it is steel and it WILL rust.

Indoor furniture, especially items like futon frames, are often made entirely of steel. You would be much better off with one made entirely of wood. If you must buy furnishings made of steel, like perhaps a hide-a-bed in which the entire mechanism is made of steel, make sure the joints and connections are all lubricated on a regular basis, or one day when you need to open it for a guest it might just be rusted solid!

Tip: when you unpack your new (or newly-moved and rust-free) appliances, apply a coat of good-quality automotive paste wax as soon as possible, and then repeat the process once a year. This makes a big difference in how long they'll last before the rust starts to show, especially on the tops of the fridges and their doors. Top surfaces of everything seem to show rust first, so keep them as well protected as you can. Of course, had the manufacturers applied a decent coat of paint at the factory or made even the teensiest effort at rust-protection, this wouldn't be necessary. In these days, however, it isn't considered good business to manufacture goods that will last longer than the warranty period, so we must take whatever steps we can to preserve them ourselves.

Stereos, TV's and other entertainment units are no more expensive here than on the Mainland, so unless you have some very nice and nearly new equipment, you might do better to sell it and replace it with new when you arrive. Electronics equipment doesn't like high humidity, and the first thing that seems to go in your entertainment equipment is the speakers. The foam rubber "surrounds" that hold the speaker cones into their frames seem to simply evaporate in short order. Some will last for years, but others will need repair or replacement in months. A lot depends on their exposure to the elements, so it's good to position your speakers (and electronics) where they do not get any direct breezes from outside. This is particularly important in the rain-forest areas where the humidity is the highest.

> Another tip: There is a product known as "ACF-50" that really works to stop corrosion. It's expensive, but the $15 spray-can goes a long way if properly applied. I found out about it in aircraft use years ago and have been using it with success around the house and on computer equipment. It's highly recommended and the manufacturer also has another product called "Corrosion Guard" which appears to be identical in performance. Check the Resource Guide for a source.

Computers and office equipment fall into the same category as electronics. We have learned to keep a dehumidifier in our office and that helps a lot. Normally, we never opt for "extended warranties," but here we have learned to buy them on computer equipment. There are numerous excellent computer businesses here that sell and service computers and peripherals at very competitive prices. It has been our experience that there is usually a very small (if any) difference in price between locally-supplied and mail-order computers and peripherals. If you factor in shipping costs and the convenience of having local support, this is an excellent case for shopping local.

Home Improvement and Remodeling

According to info on their Web site, there will be a new Home Depot in the Kailua-Kona Industrial Park by the time you read this. The existing suppliers have so far successfully lobbied to keep the Home Depot kinds of operations out for obvious reasons, but it may have finally happened. The good news is that we might be getting a Home Depot; the bad news is that it's way over there! What with East Hawai'i now being the fastest growing area in the State, it would have been ever-so-nice to have it over here, but it was not to be. But then, the whole concept is as yet only a promise, so we'll just have to wait and see.

You may be asking yourself how come we endorse Home Depot in the same chapter as we recommend shopping local. Well, we endorse shopping local if and when the local suppliers will be competitive with their pricing. To date, this has not been the case with the kinds of things we have to rely on our lumber yards and building-materials outlets to supply. They all seem to stick together on their prices, undercutting each other by pennies when they have "sales." Their prices are often so high that it is cheaper to order from the Mainland and pay the shipping charges, and to us, that indicates that they are taking advantage of a captive audience. At least Home Depot will force them (or some of them, anyway) to become more competitive.

We do a lot of remodeling, so we're looking forward to some new affordability in supplies, not to mention some new choices in products.

Vehicles

Like anyplace else, pre-owned cars are best bought from individuals rather than from dealers. For any given make, model and year vehicle, you can usually find it from a private party for way less than at any dealer, and then you save the mind-numbing experience of being put through the dealer's "system sell," not to mention the taxes and all the other creatively-inspired fees and charges. You can safely figure that a $5000 used car from a dealer will cost you an additional $700 by the time you get it out the door, most of that being the aforementioned fees and charges. And of course, you could have bought the same car for $4000 from a private party in the first place.

Car shopping here isn't much different from anywhere else, except that you need to be wary of rust that for one reason or another doesn't show. Any late-model car that is advertised as having "new paint" is suspect. Examine the car in all the places where rust shows up first and see if you can find any signs of repairs there. Look at the bottoms of the doors, around the edge of the roof, the windshield posts, around the back window and edges of the trunk (inside the trunk, too), and be sure to look under the hood. If the outside of the car looks great but under the hood is all corroded and rusty, it's likely the whole car looked bad before it was painted. Of course, if you are going to be living near the ocean where any car will rust soon, you might not care about visible rust as long as the car is in good shape mechanically. You can get some very good deals on cars like that because most people will reject the car when they see the rust.

Beyond this, use the cautions you would normally use when buying a car, and remember to never believe anything a car salesman tells you! There is a popular notion here that since this is an island and the dealers must rely on repeat customers to stay in business, that they are more likely to treat you fairly here than on the Mainland. This has not been our experience nor that of most of the people we've talked to. Yes, there are some dealers here who have good reputations and who really do treat customers as though they expect to see them again when it's time for the next car purchase. You can find these dealers by asking around. Ask folks who have lived here for years and when the same name comes up a few times, that's your dealer. Of course, this assumes that you would still rather pay more for the same car than you would have to with a private-party sale. Don't forget to add the $500-up in fabricated charges that you'll have to pay a dealer on top of the price you settle on. A fairly new trend is for dealers to charge a $200 "document fee" on every sale. There is no such legitimate thing as a document fee. It is merely one more way the dealer gets to extort an additional $200 from every customer. A "document fee" is not unlike Sears charging you $20 to write up the receipt when you make a purchase from them. Another gimmick some of our local dealers have been using is a charge for a "theft deterrent package" that just happens to already be on the vehicle you're interested in, so you have to pay for it. The so-called theft deterrent amounts to some marks that were supposedly put on the windshield so that it and/or the car itself can be identified in case of a recovered theft. I've looked at some of these vehicles and could not find any evidence of any marks on the windshield, nor does the whole concept seem valid. It's too bad that some car dealers seem to work hard to make sure that all car dealers keep their lousy reputation. Private-party sales are still the way to go.

Clothes, Etc.

Depending on your personal tastes and needs, your can cut your clothing budget to near-nothing here. In the first place, there is no need for "seasonal" attire. It's summer year 'round. See "Clothing" in Chapter 5 for more on this topic.

The Bottom Line(s)

In conclusion, let's say one more time that the most important ingredient to keeping costs down is to shop around. On any items worth more than a few dollars, never accept the first price you get. Of course, the first one might just be the cheapest once in a while, but what are the odds? Prices vary for many reasons, not limited to supply-and-demand, inventory on hand, promotional sales, and brand names. Sometimes, some of the bigger stores will make huge purchases of a few popular items and because they got them at a steal, they make them offer them as a "leader" to get people into the store. Some of the stores do this as a regular practice and once you're in the store after that single on-sale item, take notice of the rest of the prices. They might just be higher than any place else. Keep your eyes open, know what the prices are before making significant purchases. Don't assume that because a particular store has some good advertised prices that everything there will be reasonable.

Please try to shop local first. If you can find it at a locally-owned store, buy it there. Help support our local merchants, because every time the biggies put another one of them out of business, they can raise their prices accordingly. And they do. We try to keep current on the prices of things we need on a regular basis and we have noticed that some of the huge Mainland-owned "SuperStores" have consistently higher prices than some of our local shops. It's their advertised specials that draws in the crowds.

When you find a good price on non-perishable things you know you'll be needing, stock up! You might never get that price again.

With a little practice, you'll get your cost of living to a minimum and enjoy doing it.

Wailoa Park, Hilo

Chapter Seven

Income Opportunities

You may have heard that it's next to impossible to find work here. NOT! Well, let's qualify that. If you come to Hawai'i and go to the State Employment Department to ask for a job, there isn't likely to be much of a selection. In the first place, there aren't that many jobs available, and when one does come up it will more likely go to a local than to a newcomer, as well it should. But there are lots of income opportunities available to those who do not need a boss to tell them what to do next, and there are jobs available to those who excel at whatever it is they do.

Here's the Big Secret: The one thing that is in short supply here is competence in nearly any field. Which is not to say that you can't get anything done competently here; there just isn't enough competence to fill the need. If you know how to do something really well you're a dependable person willing to sell your time at a reasonable rate, there is no shortage of work. We know of no one who has a marketable skill who is looking for work. Quite the contrary; most people have more work offered than they have time for.

The job market is actually better now than it has been for many years. The high-tech sector (mostly in communications) has discovered Hawai'i Island's ideal climate and cheap real estate, and there are more companies coming in all the time. Because East Hawai'i is now the fastest-growing area of the State, the new population growth dictates the need for more housing and services, and with that, even more jobs.

Very often, we hear from somebody who is about to move back to the mainland and when we ask why, it's always the same answer: "Can't find any work here." But when we ask these people what kind of work they do, the answer is usually something like, "I'd do anything that pays a decent wage." In other words, they have no specific marketable skills; they just want "a job." These are the people who have trouble finding work and who have helped perpetuate Hawai'i's "no jobs" reputation. It's unfortunate that many parents here do not encourage their kids to have developed a marketable skill by the time they get out of high school. Many don't even have an interest, let alone a skill. For them, yes, it is hard to find work. It's not just the kids, either. We hear the same thing from adults who come move over here hoping to find work. The ones who are willing to take any kind of a job because they have no particular skill, training or the desire to create their own jobs are the ones who eventually return to the Mainland because "there is no work here."

A young man we recently spoke is an example "creating jobs." He told us he was leaving for the Mainland soon because after nearly a year of looking for work he was convinced it isn't going to happen. I asked him what kind of work he's looking for and he said he'd take anything. Further questioning revealed that he was a skilled landscape person and had worked in this field for years. We offered that there are hundreds of home-owners here who stay for a few months and live on the Mainland the rest of the year, and that he could probably keep as busy as he wanted to just doing landscape and yard maintenance for them. He made it clear that he had no interest in doing this on his own. Rather, he wanted "a job." This is a good example of what it takes for many to make it here. If you have what it takes to find a need and fill it, you will not be looking for work long. If you need a conventional job, it is much more difficult.

Consider the benefits available to the young landscape person. Working for somebody else, he has to do whatever comes along. He will be, in many cases, unable to express himself with his own special talents. He will get a wage of approximately half of what his boss charges the customers. The flip side: Working for himself, his hours are his own, his tools and equipment and all other expenses are deductible, his income is directly proportional to his effort, skill and creativity and he gets to pick and choose the jobs he wants and the days on which he chooses to do them. Food for thought.

Bring Your Hobby

A lot of retired folks here have hobbies or part-time businesses that bring in some income to supplement their retirement. Some folks we've met who have no regular retirement income have simply continued long-standing hobbies and turned them into small businesses. Others have continued whatever it was they did for a living, only scaled down to a greatly reduced pace.

We don't know of too many people here who spend their retirement years sitting in the proverbial rocking chair. There are just too many fun-and profitable-things do to with one's time.

Some Fields of Opportunity

We've got friends who are woodworkers and are busy as they wish to be (sometimes busier) trying to keep up with the demand. One neighbor makes clay jewelry in her home, is about 40, and has her beautiful home on 2 acres paid for, her car is paid for, she lives well and salts away money every month. Another neighbor opened a gallery nearby and sells the work of selected Island artists and craftspeople. She has expanded her gallery several times in the last few years and is doing very well. Her husband makes classic Island-style and exotic furniture (lots of it!) out of Koa, a beautiful indigenous Hawai'ian wood, and is always behind in his orders. Others include (very) successful photographers, fine-artists, writers, farmers, fishermen, builders, tree-trimmers, home designers, cabinet-makers, B&B owners, house-cleaners, yard-maintenance and landscaping business-owners, and owners of various stores, restaurants, and other small businesses. There are folks doing well with massage, counseling, at-home computer-based businesses, auto repair, and then there are the professionals who come here and continue their professions but at a much-reduced pace. Right now, this whole Island is in dire need for a few good, reliable cleaning services to take care of the quickly-growing vacation-rental business. Yard maintenance is another field needing capable workers. And remember, this is a tourist-destination, and although this side of the Island gets fewer tourists than the Kona side, there are still enough that there are lots of opportunities serving that population. Along that line, there's even a market here for good musicians!

A note on the tourists here, the ones who come to the Windward (Hilo) side of the Island usually have different expectations and needs than do those who go to Kona. The less-typical tourists who visit the rural and green side are more interested in things and activities that involve exploration, the arts, culture, and a non-commercial experience. There's a whole different-and interesting-market in serving folks who shy away from the typical busy tourist scene.

An opportunity that's fairly unique here is house-sitting! There are always folks who need to travel to one place or another and need dependable care of the home and possibly pets while they're away. And there are the "snowbirds," the people who own a home here and one on the Mainland and stay here during the winter months.

Some of these folks prefer not to leave their homes vacated when they are away.

These arrangements are from short-term, like a week or two, to many months. Someone with a good reputation in this field would seldom be looking for a position. This might also be the ideal setup for those who would like to live in different places all over the Island before settling on "the right one." And then the house-sitting opportunity has spawned another opportunity, as well. This happens a lot here, and creative people are starting new, innovative and successful businesses all the time. The new one here is for somebody to make up a database of people seeking and needing house-sitting services and then to connect them for a reasonable fee. Connecting people with their needs is one of the fastest-growing and most successful small businesses around, and all that's needed is a computer and a phone line. See "Some More Opportunities," below.

Staying in business

There's a saying here: "Big Island; small world." Word travels fast here, and anyone who performs his or her service with competence, dependability and integrity will get a reputation in a hurry. The laid-back Island lifestyle encourages what might appear as a flaky business attitude, so anyone who has a strong work-ethic here will be in demand!

Remember the contractor in Chapter 2 who didn't show up when he said he would because the surf was particularly good that day? Here's a variation on that one, this time for an estimate for a job, and for a specific time of day rather than a day of the week. You've been told the guy will show up at three o'clock. He shows up alright, but at five minutes to four. Well, in Hawai'ian time, if it isn't four yet, it's still three! Really! And when you think about it, it makes sense . . . kind of.

You get his price quotation, it's very reasonable and you feel good about his competence. He says he'll start tomorrow. Well, you're assuming now that because he'll start tomorrow and he said the job will take three or four days, he'll be done in three or four days, right? Not exactly. He might start tomorrow . . . and he might not. It's a surf thing. But don't be surprised if it's two weeks before he's finally done with the job.

You can usually avoid this type of thing if it's really important to you that a job be done by a certain time. You have to make that very clear up front, and some people will accept it and do the job and others will simply tell you they don't work that way. Fair enough, right?

This is like a different country and the above scenario is more the rule than the exception. It is entirely normal and expected. This scene, of course, is a generalization and it doesn't always come off this way. Sometimes people actually do exactly what they say they'll do, and even do it on time. And they, you'll find, are the ones who are never out of work.

What your trade or profession happens to be doesn't matter. There are few skills that are not needed here just as they are on the Mainland, and although there are not a lot of "jobs" available, there is always a demand for skilled help. That may seem like a curious statement, but what it boils down to is that the person who has a skill and the self discipline to be able to work on his or her own is the one who will make it here. It's the need to work for somebody else that presents a problem. There aren't a lot of employers because many of the small businesses here are so small that they run quite well with the help of a few friends or family members.

If you are fortunate to be the master of a number of skills, you would do well to check around in the area of your choice to see what skills are needed there.

And do consult the "help wanted" sections of the local papers if you're looking for any kind of professional placement. There aren't many offerings on any particular day, but they do come up on a regular basis. Dropping off resumes at businesses that seem attractive to you is another good approach. Remember, Hawai'i is a "people place," so drop them off in person.

Word travels fast on an island. If you're good at what you do, you'll soon have more work than you want. There is always a demand for the people who get a reputation for competence and dependability.

The Arts

We've amazed several of our visiting mainland artist friends when we introduced them to our friends here who are supporting themselves quite well with their art. The more common scene on the mainland is that artists must have a "real job" to support their art!

The arts and crafts field is alive and well here and supports many people quite nicely. The ones who seem to do the best are those who have developed a genuine feel for Hawai'i, her people and her magic. Their art reflects this feeling and when it comes through as genuine, it sells well not only to tourists, but to locals as well. It's interesting to go to some of the many events that feature crafts booths and look at the offerings. After doing this for a while, you can get a clear picture of what sells well and what does not. Quality and craftsmanship are definitely important; the buying public does know the difference! It is also interesting to see all of the innovation and creativity displayed at these events. Just when you think that there can't be any more original ideas, you'll be surprised with some more.

Here's yet another opportunity related to the arts field. We know of several artisans and writers who would jump at the opportunity to have somebody represent them and their work at the many galleries and other outlets around the Islands. Sales and promotion have always been huge obstacles to success for artists, writers and crafts people. Most do not have the time, expertise or the inclination to handle their own promotion and distribution, so their work often stays unsold. Simply getting it out there, exposing it to the many venues available here, would make all the difference.

We also know of one very successful photographer who makes his own trips to all of the galleries and shops that handle his work on all of the Islands. He does this because he has not been able to find anyone who will represent his work a manner consistent with his needs. His needs are simple: a bright, enthusiastic person who is both dependable and trustworthy. There are not even any sales involved here; just doing the rounds to check inventories and to help the various merchants with their restocking orders. A commission of 25% would be reasonable to pay for this work, plus additional commissions for any new accounts. Who would be your clients for this kind of service? A big percentage of all the artists and crafts people in Hawai'i. Of course, this would only work for somebody who would enjoy making monthly tax-deductible trips around the Islands . . . Opportunities abound!

Some More Opportunities

We also know of several people who have made successes of computer-based home businesses. They simply found different people who had a need to be connected, and they became the liaisons. We know of a woman who started an Internet vacation-rental listing service, and before her first year in business, she had over 1000 listings. She charged a very-affordable

$100/year to her clients, put each listing on an attractive Web page, and that's all she needs do from there on in. She collects $100/year from each client each year for the continued listings, the clients are thrilled to receive world-wide advertising for their rentals for such a low price, and everybody is happy. She now has several thousand listings at $100/year . . . do the math! Above, we mentioned the possibility of connecting house-sitting people with others needing their services. Once a core business is established on this Island, it can easily be expanded to the other Islands as well, and from there to other vacation destinations around the world. Think of the perks: deductible vacations around the world to check out new sites for development of your business!

Another friend runs aquarobics instruction at a local public pool and at a close-by huge, geothermally-heated tidepool. Not a bad way to earn a living! The tourist trade here also brings us other options, including vacation-rental needs ranging from the rentals themselves to management, booking and maintenance (badly-needed, too); wedding co-ordinators and related businesses; and of course, food service opportunities that are limited only by one's imaginations.

Vacation Rentals

You're probably familiar with vacation rentals. Instead of staying in a tiny hotel room for $150 a night, you rent a home or condo for less money and you have your own little home-away-from-home. They are truly a win-win situation for everybody.

In recent months, the purchase of vacation rentals has become very popular here and for good reason. Here's an example: You find a small house or condo, well situated for vacationers. This means it's either on the ocean, has an ocean view, or is close to some desirable tourist amenities. You buy the house or condo for say, $100,000. Now if this was a month-to-month rental, you could expect a return of $600/month. But as a vacation rental, your income will be closer to $2500 a month. Not a bad return on your investment! Of course, there are expenses. You'll have to pay for cleanings, maintenance, taxes, utilities, advertising and perhaps a booking agent if that is your choice. But typically, you can buy a $100,000 home here and even with a healthy mortgage you can expect a solid positive cash-flow every month.

A caution: We have been seeing some people want to jump on they perceive to be an "easy-money" bandwagon. They'll buy a house in shabby condition, throw on a coat of paint and call it a "vacation rental." Please don't even consider this business unless you are willing to offer your guests a premium product. Your vacation home must be prepared with *Aloha* and must be in excellent condition inside and out. The furnishings, appliances, linens and other appointments must be well kept, everything must work properly, and the place has to speak to your guests that you care about them and their enjoyable vacation in Hawai'i.

When our vacation rental guests arrive at their homes, the places sparkle! There are fresh flowers, some tropical treats, a welcome note and some nice, quiet Hawai'ian music in the air. They feel the *Aloha* the minute they arrive, and they usually let us know about it, too.

This fairly new business opportunity brings with it the needs for more business opportunities, too There are individuals here who "do cleanings," but few seem to be very professional. As with a lot of other services here, they are available but it's hard to find competent and dependable people. Somebody could start a cleaning service, then hire help as the contracts come in. After a few more contracts, the business owner would become the manager who oversees those who are actually doing the work. This can be a lucrative business, and as with all other such small businesses, it can be expanded into spinoff services. A cleaning service could sub-contract other services, making a profit from each. Carpet cleaning, interior painting and decorating, supplying consumables and even small appliances and furnishings as needed, handyman and any other related services are all possibilities. Remember, many vacation-rental owners live on the Mainland and would just love to have one person to depend on for all of their long-distance needs.

The possibilities here really are just about endless!

A story

This morning my bride, Camille, was on the phone with a young woman somewhere on the Mainland. Camille was ordering something out of a catalog, and when the woman took down our address, she started in on what was it like to live in Hawai'i, and then all the subsequent questions. She told Camille that she was in administrative work and would she be able to find work here? Well, Because we get these kinds of questions often, We tossed around how we could address this topic in the book. What we came up with was that most of the people we know who are in administrative work seem to be doing it as a means to and end rather than as a vocation of choice. Many administrative positions pay well, especially in the big cities, and the pay is the reason for being there. Many of them also carry more than their share of responsibility, headaches and heartaches. It seems somehow out of alignment to us, then, to think of coming to this place of peace and magic and to bring along such a stressful lifestyle-unless, of course, it is something that you genuinely enjoy doing.

One of the big problems with many administrative or even executive positions is that there is never any sense of completion. This isn't just an accident, either, but is designed into many such jobs. The corporations know that when they get an employee with a strong work-ethic and who is driven to succeed, that person will respond in a predictable manner to a job with no sense of completion. The result is often an employee who will work extra hours for no extra pay, all in a never-ending effort to excel at a job in which there are no wins. The job never ends, it never comes to a point where the employee can kick back and feel good about his or her accomplishment. Whatever he or she does is never quite good enough, and the rat-race goes on until there's a breakdown of some sort.

To those of you who are just doing it because it pays well, we would like to respectfully recommend considering changing careers! Scary? Yes, maybe it is. But we'd bet that the more thought you give the idea, the less intimidating it will feel. Whatever you job or vocation is, if it's something you're doing only because the pay is good and you'd really prefer doing something else, do it! We've known doctors and highly-paid executives who have given up a lucrative practice in exchange for some serious inner peace in the form of a simple lifestyle of love and harmony with nature. We've also met some who have simply given up a busy and hectic big-city practice, moved here and started a limited, part-time practice that they could pursue with a glad heart.

Remember, no more staff payroll or the attendant insurance and other overhead. Here, the lifestyle is so different from "big city" that the costs dwindle to a manageable amount, leaving the same net income with a lot less gross income.

Even the costs of having one of those high-paying jobs in the big city are significant. Consider the new car, the fancy clothes, the time spent commuting, social obligations—it all adds up. All of a sudden you can work close to home—or maybe even at home, your commuting costs have gone away, your clothing budget is now nearly zip, you now have the time you used to waste sitting in traffic to spend with your kids (or at the beach), and you don't need the Lexus any more.

In choosing a career or even just a job, it is much better to decide first what fulfills us—what we enjoy doing, and then find work in that area than the more usual approach of "going where the money is." After all, what we're all after in the end is peace of mind and happiness. Very few people who work just for the big bucks have much of either.

About That Lexus

The fancy-car thing is another interesting phenomenon here. On the Mainland, people tend to make assessments of our station in life, our credibility and more, by what we drive up in. And of course, on the long commute to work, we pass by innumerable conspicuous offerings of shiny new cars, constantly reminding us that what we have is not quite good enough. Being well-trained consumers, this influence tends to work, too. When we arrive at work we have to park amongst all the shiny, impressive new cars and we certainly can't be outdone there, either.

Here, nobody cares what you drive up in. Whether you show up in a Mercedes Limo or a rusty old pickup simply does not matter. It's hard for a lot of newcomers to get this, but sooner or later, even the those most dedicated to their image tend to shed that feeling, and best of all, it's really a psychologically and spiritually healthy place to be.

"Where the Money Is"

We talk to friends and relatives who live in the Silicon Valley, one of the most expensive places in the country to reside. We ask them why is it so important to them to live in a place that is so hopelessly overcrowded, so incredibly expensive; where the smog is so thick it's hard to see buildings a few blocks away and the lifestyle is so frenetic; where sirens scream and tires screech, horns blare and car-alarms are going off everywhere, where most conversation centers around stock options and where nobody seems to have time for anything worthwhile? The universal answer? "THAT'S WHERE THE MONEY IS!"

OK, let's do some simple math here. We know a few couples there who have to *bring home* well over $100,000 a year just to pay the expenses. No frills, just the bills. To bring home $100,000 after taxes, they need a combined gross income of far more than that. So they both have to work at full-time jobs so they can afford to live "where the money is."

We also know families who live very comfortably here in Paradise on $35,000 a year, and they make it with one income and have lots of free time to spend with family and friends, at the beach, going on trips, whatever. And many of the families here will be living in homes much nicer than those in the most expensive places in the country to live.

It's all in one's priorities, it seems. It's always been our feeling that it is essential to first find the place where you would like most to live, and then figure out how to support yourself there. Most folks tend to go where they think they can earn the most money, and then try to figure out how to be happy there. Unfortunately, the places with the traditionally high incomes are also the places with the traditionally high cost of living, the most crime, pollution, traffic problems and other elements interfering with one's peace.

Another Little Story

Our dear son, now 25 and recently married, moved to California's Silicon Valley and landed one of those sweet jobs in the computer industry. In his four years there so far, he's already had several pay raises and now makes a bundle of money—far more than his parents have ever made! His bride works at a good paying job, too. On their combined income, they're having a hard time staying on top of their expenses. Our son recently told us that he figured out that the big-bucks jobs aren't what they're cracked up to be. After all the taxes they have to pay on such an income, they are left with a little more than half of what they earn, and that gets handily consumed by the outrageous rent and all of the other incredible expenses of living there. He said that at the cost of living here in Hawai'i, they could live better here on half of what they're earning there. This isn't an isolated example, either. Lots of people are in similar positions, if they'd only do the math. In their case, though, they're young and for now at least, they like the pace of life there so it's worth it to them. We feel blessed that they are able to see—and talk about— the whole dismal picture of being stuck in what is so aptly called the ratrace. They are enjoying it for what they can get out of it now, but have no intention to make it their way of life. We just hope they come back home one day.

In Conclusion

One of the unique things about living in Hawai'i is that first of all, if this is your Paradise (as it certainly is for many), you can earn any amount of money you desire here. If you are even a little bit creative, your income can be directly proportional to your effort. But then, if you have no aspirations to earn lots of money but just want to live a quiet, carefree and beautiful life in the tropics, you can do what we did: figure out what kind of a lifestyle you can afford on however much you know you can easily bring in. We developed our simple lifestyle around our more-or-less fixed retirement income and it's working ever so well. The only time we need hustle up additional funds is for extras, like travel or major purchases. And then we have several income-producing avocations in which we enjoy dabbling when the need arises. We live in a modest-but-beautiful home in a tiny community, within sight and sound of the ocean. At this moment, I'm sitting on our lanai with my laptop, enjoying warm, sensuous tropical breezes as I "work." Two laptops, actually. The other one is our kitty, Lucy, who loves to help me type.

Distant views on the Kailua Coast are often partially obscured in volcanic haze (vog).

Chapter Eight

Retirement Opportunities

Retirement in Hawai'i! What a concept! And for those folks lucky enough to have a fairly big equity in their Mainland homes, retirement in Hawai'i is a cinch! Did you buy a Mainland home years ago that is now either paid off or has a big equity, even if only due to the inflation over the years? We know of quite a few people who've sold those homes and bought one here for a small portion of the proceeds and then retired on the change. Sounds good? How does that work?

Well, let's start at the low end of the possibilities. Let's say that your home is paid for and is now worth $300,000. Not much by Mainland standards, right? So you sell the house, buy one for $100,000 here and live off of the proceeds of the well-invested balance. Or if you're so inclined, invest some of the balance in a small business that you can thoroughly enjoy running on a part-time basis.

So now you're asking, "How can you possibly live off of the interest on a $200,000 investment?" It's not difficult to get a return of well over $1000 a month on that kind of an investment, and if you add that to any small retirement income or even your Social Security payments, you will have enough to live quite well in Hawai'i (in your paid-for home). No, you won't be buying expensive toys or flying to America to see the kids every few months, but it will cover your living expenses. What we do is have several little enterprises going on that bring in small amounts of income each, and if we need a bigger infusion of cash for something outside our budget, we just put in a little more time to earn the money. Our rule is to avoid spending our investment principal.

Again, well over $1000 a month is easy on an investment of $200,000. Now if you'd like to get a little bit creative, you can do a whole lot better than that. Among other options explored in the preceding chapter, the real-estate market rebound is on the ground floor now, offering many investment opportunities.

The above situation applies to folks of retirement age. So you say you're ready to retire and you're nowhere near old enough to receive Social Security? If you quit your job, can you cash in a nice portfolio of stock options? Well, if you can't, you'll have to tap other resources. Among them are home equity, savings, and of course, earning a retirement income once you get here. See Chapter 7 for lots of possibilities.

Living in a world-class tourist destination gives us many income possibilities not available elsewhere. One intriguing opportunity that is described in Chapter 7 is vacation rentals. This is an ideal income producer for retired folks with a little investment capital, and it doesn't take much to get started. You can manage your rental yourself, as we do, or use an agent. There are agents here who manage these homes, and that includes doing the advertising, bookings and arranging cleanings and necessary maintenance. They usually charge 15% to 20% of the total rents, and of course you get billed for the cleanings and maintenance. (Some charge up to 50%, so ask around!) You could either buy a vacation rental a few years before actually moving over and have it already earning for you, or wait until you arrive for good. Another option for vacation rentals is to buy a home with a nice apartment or *ohana* to use as a vacation rental. Of course, such a home would have to be in a vacation-desirable location. With even a modest down payment on a carefully-selected property, there is still a solid positive cash flow after all the expenses. This works well no matter when you actually plan on moving here for good.

Vacation-rental homes on the Hilo side

Each of these opportunities seem to spawn its own sideline possibilities, and many of them are perfectly suited to the retiree. Some, like agenting vacation rentals, can furnish the entrepreneur with exactly the desired amount of work and income. You list however many vacation homes you feel comfortable handling and don't accept any more than that. There are plenty to go around, so you even have your choice of which ones you would like to handle. See Chapter 7 for more on this enticing business opportunity.

If you have $200,000 left from the sale of your Mainland home after you purchase your home here, that could provide you with an easy $3,000 per month (after all expenses are paid) income from well-purchased vacation rentals.

Here's one of ours as an example: We bought a humble little ocean-front house for $97,000 and spent about $8,000 on it for remodeling and furnishing. The place is now beautiful and gets rave reviews from our guests, who are thrilled to pay $75 a night to call it home for their vacations. We took out a $40,000 mortgage and the payments are $370. Taxes, utilities, insurance and all other expenses bring our total expenses to about $800 per month and the income averages $2,000. So, for our cash investment of $75,000 we have a consistent net income of about $1200 per month. In a few months, our rental rate will increase to $85, bringing the income up by another $250-300 per month. We could also have mortgaged the house for more than we did, thus freeing up more capital for another purchase, and still had a healthy positive cash flow.

Another income from this investment is that this little house that we've got $105,000 invested in is now worth about $140,000, not even a year later. A further, less obvious income is that we can depreciate the house and its contents on our taxes, thereby lowering the tax liability on our income.

Please keep in mind what we said earlier about the apparent "easy-money" in vacation rentals: Forget it unless you're prepared to offer an exemplary product.

Many people who have held a straight job for a lot of years also have a monthly retirement check to add to their income, and those over 62 can collect their Social Security payments, as well. None of these by themselves might be significant, but we like living on the "trickle of nickels" system. Nice thing about it is that if one trickle dries up for a while, there are always the others. It just feels a lot more secure to us than to depend on one source of income for all our needs.

Remember, we're talking about the low end of possibilities here, and the kind of lifestyle possible on this minimal kind of an income suits a lot of people very well. Living on less works well in Hawai'i anyway, because when you're here, all of your priorities will shift. New cars and flashy houses just don't seem to matter any longer, nor do stylish fashions or any of hundreds of other drains that normal city-folks have on their incomes. Here, life is about people; friends and family, and the strangers who are just friends you haven't met yet. You'll find yourself spending more time floating in a warm, clear tide pool and less time at cocktail parties; more time at your neighbor's house "talking story" and less time rushing from place to busy place; more time at a comfortable and interesting farmer's market and less time in crowded, noisy (and expensive) supermarkets; and most important, more time at peace with yourself and your environment and less time in the day-to-day struggles so pervasive in city life.

If you have the inclination to start up a small business in Hawai'i, the possibilities are exciting and seem endless. We are constantly amazed by the new and innovative ideas people keep coming up with.

Since you most likely won't need the kind of income you have become used to, you might even consider expanding your favorite pastime or hobby into a business opportunity!

OK, that calls for a little explanation. If we're sounding a bit presumptuous telling you what kind of an income you won't need here, let us again emphasize that this book is written specifically for the folks who are in love with Hawai'i and are looking for an affordable life here. Affordable, by our standards, means a $300,000 home is out of the question. Affordable, by our standards, means a total cost of living of under $2000 a month. And for some, a lot less than that.

There are other books on relocating to Hawai'i that are written for folks of means; the people to whom a $300,000 house is a "starter home." It's unlikely you're in that category since you're still reading this book!

In conclusion, the many friends we've made here who have done just what we've shared in this chapter are living proof that it is not only possible, but even easy. All that is needed is the desire and a little creative planning. After all, we did it, and we like to think of ourselves as beach bums.

Of course, we also have friends still on the Mainland who keep telling us how they are "trapped" there and how much they would love to be able to do what we're doing. We patiently tell them exactly how they could pull it off, but they have all these reasons why it just wouldn't work for them. We believe what's really missing for them is the desire.

The bottom line: Our calendar has a "quote for the day" for each day of the year. This morning's quote: "What I truly value, I do." That says it all.

A Volcano Village home

Chapter Nine

Health Care in Hawai'i

The Hawai'i Medical Service Association (HMSA) is the largest provider of health care coverage in the state, and is a nonprofit, mutual benefit society founded in 1938. They provide health plans and employee benefit services. HMSA is led by an executive staff and governed by a 27-member, consumer-oriented board of directors. The board represents a broad cross-section of the local community, including government, business, labor, management, education, finance, the medical profession, religion and the general public. HMSA is a member of the Blue Cross and Blue Shield Association, an association of independent Blue Cross and Blue Shield plans.

Kaiser Permanente is the largest federally qualified, nonprofit HMO in the country and introduced affordable comprehensive coverage to Hawaii residents in 1958 and now serves more than 215,000 members at the Moanalua Medical Center and 22 clinics on four islands, including two on the Big Island.

Kaiser Permanente Hawaii was among only 40 plans out of over 650 HMOs in the United States to receive the prestigious "excellent" accreditation status from the National Committee for Quality Assurance (NCQA).

NCQA is an independent, not-for-profit organization dedicated to assessing and reporting on the quality of managed care plans. (NCQA "excellent" accreditation applies to Kaiser Permanente HMO plans.)

Kaiser Permanente Hawai'i is also accredited by: The Joint Commission on Accreditation of Healthcare Organizations (JCAHO) for their hospital, skilled nursing facility, and home care program; the American College of Radiology for their mammography facilities; and the College of American Pathologists for our laboratories.

Other awards received by Kaiser Permanente include:

'Oihana Maika'i, 1996, Kaiser Permanente received the Hawaii State Award of Excellence to recognize our outstanding commitment to excellence in areas including customer service and satisfaction.

Pulama 'Ohana Award, 1996, Kaiser Permanente received this award to recognize how we care for, cherish, and nurture the family.

Island Business' "Investing in the Environment" Award, 1996.

Our personal experience with Kaiser Permanente Hawaii has been excellent in all areas. We like the fact that most services and procedures are covered 100% instead of the usual coverages limited to some percentage of whatever an "approved" amount happens to be, leaving you to pay a large portion of every bill. With Kaiser, there's never a need to figure out the coverages that seem to vary with each service from most providers. When a patient needs care medical attention that is beyond the scope of the Big Island's two clinics, Kaiser Permanente flies the patient at their expense to the Moanalua Center on Oahu.

Please visit the Web sites listed in the Resource Guide for a complete look at the above medical resources, plus some valuable info on Hawaii's medical services in general.

The magical "Red Road" on the Puna coast

Chapter Ten

Final Thoughts

We've covered a lot of ground in these chapters and have had fun doing it. If we've left you more sure about your feelings on moving to Hawai'i, we're thrilled. Actually, whether you're more sure than ever that Hawai'i will be your new home, or if we've helped you discover that you now would like to rethink the whole idea, it doesn't matter. What is important is that we've helped you become clear on your intentions.

It has been our experience that once we get very clear on what it is we're after, it all seems to fall into place. Every time. On the flip side, if we're confused, can't make up our minds one way or the other, or are even the slightest bit unsure, it's a fight all the way and the odds are stacked against success.

We recommend that in these kinds of decisions, you listen to your heart—your intuition. Sure, there are lots of practical, nuts-and-bolts choices that need to be made when considering a major lifestyle change like this, but the final word should come from a place other than logic. The final decision is not a logical one because moving to Hawai'i is indeed a major lifestyle change. It's not at all comparable to moving from one Mainland state to another, even though that could be a big deal, as well.

At this point, you should have a good feeling of why we say Hawai'i is a lot like a foreign country. As soon as you get settled in and start to allow your life to expand past your personal world and that of your immediate new friends, neighbors and maybe your new work environment, you'll soon find out that everything works differently here. It is widely understood here that Hawai'i embraces some people and rejects others. We hope that we have given you the tools with which to assess your own Island-Life compatibility.

What we have shared with you here is basic inside information from those who have gone before you. It's a glimpse into the future, with somebody else having taken the bumps for you.

Whether or not you ultimately decide to make Hawai'i your own Paradise, it is our sincere hope that we've been of help with your decisions. But even more so, if you decide Hawai'i will be your home, we hope we've given you some valuable tools to help with your adventure!

Wherever life leads you, we wish you brilliant rainbows, spectacular sunsets and much *Aloha*!

Aloha Nui Loa!

Skip Thomsen
and the Thomsen Ohana

AFFORDABLE PARADISE

Resource Guide

Newspapers

West Hawai'i Today is Kailua-Kona's Newspaper.
Web site: *www.WestHawaiiToday.com*
Mail contact: Attention: Circulation Department
P.O. Box 789 Kailua-Kona, Hawai'i 96745-0789
For more information: Circulation Department,
808-329-9311

Hawai'i Tribune Herald is Hilo's Newspaper.
Web site: *www.HiloHawaiiTribune.com/*
Subscription Information: E-mail:
subscriptions@hawaiitribuneherald.com

Note: Both of the above newspapers have their
classified sections on their Web sites.

Hawai'i Island Journal is Hawai'i Island's
independent newspaper.
P.O. Box 7179, Ocean View, Hawai'i 96737
Subscription information: 808-328-1951. E-
mail: *subscribe@hawaiijournal.com*
Hawai'i Island Journal has our recommendation
for its straightforward, unbiased reporting of
many Island issues, including political,

environmental and more. Included in each issue
is a comprehensive calendar of all kinds of
events, Island-wide. It's a free paper, found just
about anywhere on the Island. Subscriptions are
mailed anywhere.

Real Estate Resources

Hawaii Information.com
Here's the best, all-inclusive Web site for all of
your real-estate needs. Check it out and you will
be amazed!
www.hawaiiinformation.com

Hilo Brokers: An excellent Real Estate info resource
for East Hawai'i: Check out their informative
Web site: *www.hilobrokers.com*

West Hawai'i (Kona side) **Realtors Web Site**: This
excellent Web site features a number of different
Realtors, all on the Kona side.
www.konaweb.com/real

Two Web sites exclusively for FSBO's
(For Sale By Owner):
www.fsbo-world.com/
www.homeportfoliojunction.com/home/
Hawaii.htm

Other Real Estate Web sites: Type "Big Island real estate," "Hilo real estate," "Big Island for sale by owner," or whatever your imagination inspires into your favorite search utility. Get specific on location if you are interested in only that part of the Island. There are many excellent Web sites covering all areas of the Island.

Tax Records Web Site: This site will give you all of the records available at the property tax office in Hilo, and right on your own PC! *www.hawaiipropertytax.com*

County Tax Office

(For info on possible real estate purchases) These folks have a computer available to the public on which you can locate any parcel of land on the Island. All you need is the TMK number.
865 Pi'ilani Street, Hilo, Hawai'i 96720.
1-808-961-8282
See also: www.*hawaiipropertytax.com*

Lenders

City Bank is a mortgage broker that has received excellent referrals from numerous people. We have worked with them ourselves and received professional, competent and friendly service.
City Bank, Mortgage Department
808-934-9836
586 Kanoelehua, Suite 205
Hilo, HI 96720

Charter Funding is another mortgage broker that does no-doc loans and will work with non-resident buyers.
1-808-935-7500.
75-170 Hualalai Rd. Suite B-102
Kailua-Kona, Hawai'i 96740.

More Real Estate Resources

Homes & Land. A full-color magazine showing real estate listings all over the Island. It's available free in racks outside of restaurants, grocery stores and elsewhere. You can also see their listings at www.homes.com. If you'd like your own free copy, call 1-800-277-7800.

Title Guaranty Escrow Services We recommend these folks' very professional and competent services for your real estate needs: 450 Kilauea Ave., Hilo, Hawai'i 96720. 1-808-935-6638.

Home Inspections

Orchid Isle Home Inspection Eric Cohen, owner of OIHI, works with the buyer or seller, does full or partial inspections of homes, condos and commercial buildings. 808-965-9022, E-mail: *dandecohen@earthlink.net*

Hawai'i Island Street Guides

East Hawai'i Street Guide
>Record Copy Service
>P.O. Box 11173
>Hilo, Hawai'i 96721
>(808) 935-0092
>E-mail: *cbm@ilhawaii.net*

West Hawai'i Street Guide
>Swordfish Island Enterprises
>75-5595 Palani Rd.,Box #6-152
>Kailua-Kona, Hawai'i 96740 (808) 325-6643

The above Street Guides are excellent, cover every street with detailed maps, and also list all of the residential subdivisions by name and location. Well worth the money if you're planning on doing a lot of house-hunting! They are available at most book stores and other locations, as well. The cost is about $10.

Vacation-Rental Web Sites
If you would rather stay in a nicely-furnished home than in a hotel room (for the same price), check out these Web sites:
www.A1KapohoVacation.com
www.vrbo.com (Vacation Rentals by Owners)
www.vacationhomes.com

Each of these Web sites has listings of vacation rentals ranging from humble to luxurious.

Simply click your way to the Big Island, and then to the specific location you desire. Another good way to find more sites is to simply type into a search engine the location (Hilo, Puna, etc.) you would like to stay, along with the words vacation rental.

Other Resources

Hawaii Charter Schools website
http://www.k12.hi.us/~bwoerner/hacs/index.html

Moving Guide: *So You Want to Live in Hawai'i*
by Toni Polancy.
Ms Polancy's book has lots of good nuts-and-bolts info on relocating to Hawai'i. In our opinions, she addresses well-to-do people who would prefer the upscale regions of Maui to rural Hawai'i, but the moving logistics are the same regardless of your Island destination. The book is a good resource. Available from Amazon.com or your local book store.

Shipping

Matson Navigation 1-800-4-MATSON
For your Mainland-to-Hawai'i shipping needs. Visit their excellent Web site for any info you might need about shipping your belongings and vehicles. *www.matson.com*

Mihira Transfer 1-808-935-1597

For your Big Island shipping needs. We've had excellent, prompt, courteous and reasonable service from these folks. We recommend them for shipping your container from the Hilo dock to your new home.

DHX Dependable Hawaiian Express

1-800-488-4888 (Local: 933-7780)

These folks ship between the Islands and Seattle, Portland, Oakland and LA. They will ship either full or partial containers and you have the choice of furnishing your own transport between the docks and your home or they'll go door-to-door. A great solution for you if you don't need a whole container. We've used them for efficient and dependable less-than-container sized shipments.

Doing Business in Hawai'i

Business Basics in Hawai'i: Secrets of Starting Your Own Business in Our State, by Dennis K. Kondo. Available from Amazon.com or your local book store.

Motor Vehicles Office/Information: 1-808-961-8351

Phone Companies

Verizon Hawai'i:
Website: *www.verizon.net*, and
www.verizon.com
Questions, or ordering a phone book: 1-808-643-3456. Also for ordering phone books: P.O. Box 2200, Honolulu, HI 96841

Cellular service: AT&T. This is the only Cellular service that at this time works in all (well, almost all) areas of the Island. 1-888-289-8722. Local Hilo Store: 333 Kilauea Ave., Hilo, HI 96720. 808-935-9749

Library

Hilo Public Library (Great resource for real estate TMK maps.)
300 Waianuenue Avenue, Hilo, Hawai'i 96720. 1-808-933-8888 The library's entire State-wide catalog is available (the same screen as you get on the library's own computers) with a modem connection to 1-808-982-4436. A real plus!

Rust Protection!

"ACF-50" Here's a product everyone living in Hawai'i should know about: "ACF-50," also sold as "Corrosion Guard." Use it on all of your rust-prone belongings as soon as you get them here! It absolutely stops corrosion if properly applied to new metal, and stops the spread of corrosion when applied to old metal. It's available from Alumside Products, Inc., 20 Kukila Street, Hilo, Hawai'i 96720. 1-808-935-5485. You can find other retailers by calling: 1-800-256-2548.

Pet Info

Animal Quarantine Information
The State of Hawai'i's Animal Quarantine Laws: *www.mauibuyersbroker.com/transportation/animal.html*
State of Hawai'i Department of Agriculture

Animal Quarantine Station
99-951 Halawa Valley Street
Aiea, Hawai'i 96701
Telephone (808) 488-8461
www.maui.net/~paradise/events/MHS/Mauihumane.html

General Hawai'i Information Resource

www.konaweb.com has a wealth of info, including a forum about moving to the Big Island. The Web site is heavily biased toward the Kona side, but there's still a lot of good info that applies to the whole Island. Among the topics covered:

Hawai'i Health Information Corporation
http://www.hhic.org/index.html

Hawai'i Health Information Corporation
http://www.hhic.org/healthtrends/
healthtrends.html

HMSA, the largest health care provider in Hawai'i
http://www.hmsa.com/

Kaiser Permanente Hawai'i
http://www.kaiserpermanente.org/
locations/hi/

AFFORDABLE PARADISE

About the Author

Skip Thomsen was born and raised in the San Francisco Bay Area and has had an avid interest in writing since childhood. He has written and successfully self-published several books over the last twelve years.

Marketing for his self-published titles is through his company, Oregon Wordworks, in Portland, Oregon.

He has also written numerous magazine articles on various how-to topics, including some on relocating to Hawai'i. Reviews of his writing consistently commend him for his ability to make complex topics clear and easy to understand.

During 1988-89, he and his then-wife published an arts-and-entertainment guide called *Elixir!* for the North Oregon Coast area. A paper of 16-20 pages with a circulation of five-thousand copies, it included a variety of articles, fiction, and poetry concerning Oregon Coast issues. It was well received, got great reviews and supported itself from the start with enthusiastic local advertisement. It was put to sleep when Skip moved to Hawai'i in 1993.

Thomsen spent the better part of three years in Hawai'i in the early seventies and knew for certain that this is where he wanted to spend the rest of his life. Circumstances prompted his move back to the Mainland, but the dream of some day moving to Hawai'i never left him. In 1993, he visited the Islands on his way home from a trip to New Zealand, and for the first time discovered how inexpensive housing was on the Big Island. During that visit, he bought a home there and within a few months had moved to Hawai'i for good.

For these last nine years, friends, visitors, tourists and acquaintances have been making comments like, "How can you afford to live in Hawai'i full time? Isn't it awfully expensive?" To their amazement, Skip and his wife, Camille would tell them that they live in the Islands for less than the cost of their modest lifestyles on the Mainland. Of course, everyone wanted to know all the details. Some even recommended Skip write a book on the subject!

There continues to be such a conspicuous amount of interest in affordable living in Hawai'i that the natural next step was *Affordable Paradise.* The first printing sold out quickly and the new material included in this second printing was mostly in response to feedback from the enthusiastic readers of the original book.

Index

Additional copies of

Affordable Paradise

May be ordered direct from the publisher.
Please send a check or money order
For $12.95 plus $2 S&H to:
OREGON WORDWORKS
P.O. Box 231091
Portland, OR 97281

Internet Credit-Card orders from
The Affordable Paradise Website:

www.AffordableHawaiiLiving.com

or simply call
1-800-431-1579
for toll-free credit-card phone orders

**Affordable Paradise is also available at
your local bookstore or from Amazon.com**